THE
AURORA
INTERSTELLAR
COLLECTIVE

An Interdimensional Galleria

Images, Messages and Evidence of
The Beings of Light Among Us

GIA GOVINDA MARIE

SACRED DRAGON PUBLISHING
LOS ANGELES, CA

Sacred Dragon Publishing Services LLC™
Los Angeles, California

SacredDragonPublishing.com
 ISBN: 978-1-967005-00-0 Paperback
 ISBN: 978-1-967005-01-7 Hardcover

Cover and Interior Design: Amygdala Design

Printed in the United States of America.

ACKNOWLEDGEMENTS

ETERNAL THANKS to The Most Radiant One, my beloved Angels, the Nature Spirits, Beings of Light, Ascended Masters, Aurora, and benevolent Cosmic Guides who have walked beside me and guided me through my evolution on the Earth.

TO MY EARTHLY ANGELS, my beloved friends and family, who stepped forward in my time of greatest need, leaving offerings at my door as I climbed the tumultuous terrain toward the summit. May your cups runneth over with blessings always.

SPECIAL THANKS to Chris H. for his patience, technological savviness and expertise, continually available to lend a helping hand.

LOVING BLESSINGS to Mother Earth for holding the energetic field for humanity to Awaken, and for cradling me in her loving care from the beginning of my incarnation on this plane.

UNENDING LOVE to my beloved shepherd Gandalf, my faithful White Knight, who was my touchstone to life through this experience, never leaving my side and traveling everywhere with me. And to my beautiful shepherd Thorin, my ethereal White Knight. May you ALWAYS know how much you are treasured as you roam the meadows of Spirit and continue to work with me from above. My love for you is never ending!

INFINITELY & FOREVER, to my precious daughter, Camille, a true gift from God, who graciously bestows magical blessings upon me daily as we journey together on this Earth. You are my shining star, and words cannot begin to express my infinite love for you!

DEDICATION

To my Beloved AURORA,
the Nature Spirits and Beings of Light.
Thank you for sharing your luminous light with the world,
as we journey together beyond the veil of The Golden Age,
and co-create A New Earth.

This Interdimensional Galleria
gifts humanity with tangible evidence of
The Beings of Light Among Us, beautifully bridging
SCIENCE & SPIRITUALITY
like never before, as we enter the new Era of Terra,
and Mother Earth makes her much anticipated and long-awaited
Grand Alignment in the Stars.

As you peruse these pages,
you receive divine downloads,
awakening dormant codes and filaments of light within,
igniting ancient memories of the RADIANT BEING that you are
and your assignment of duty
on this Earth.

TABLE OF CONTENTS

Part 3: Aurora's Interdimensional Galleria

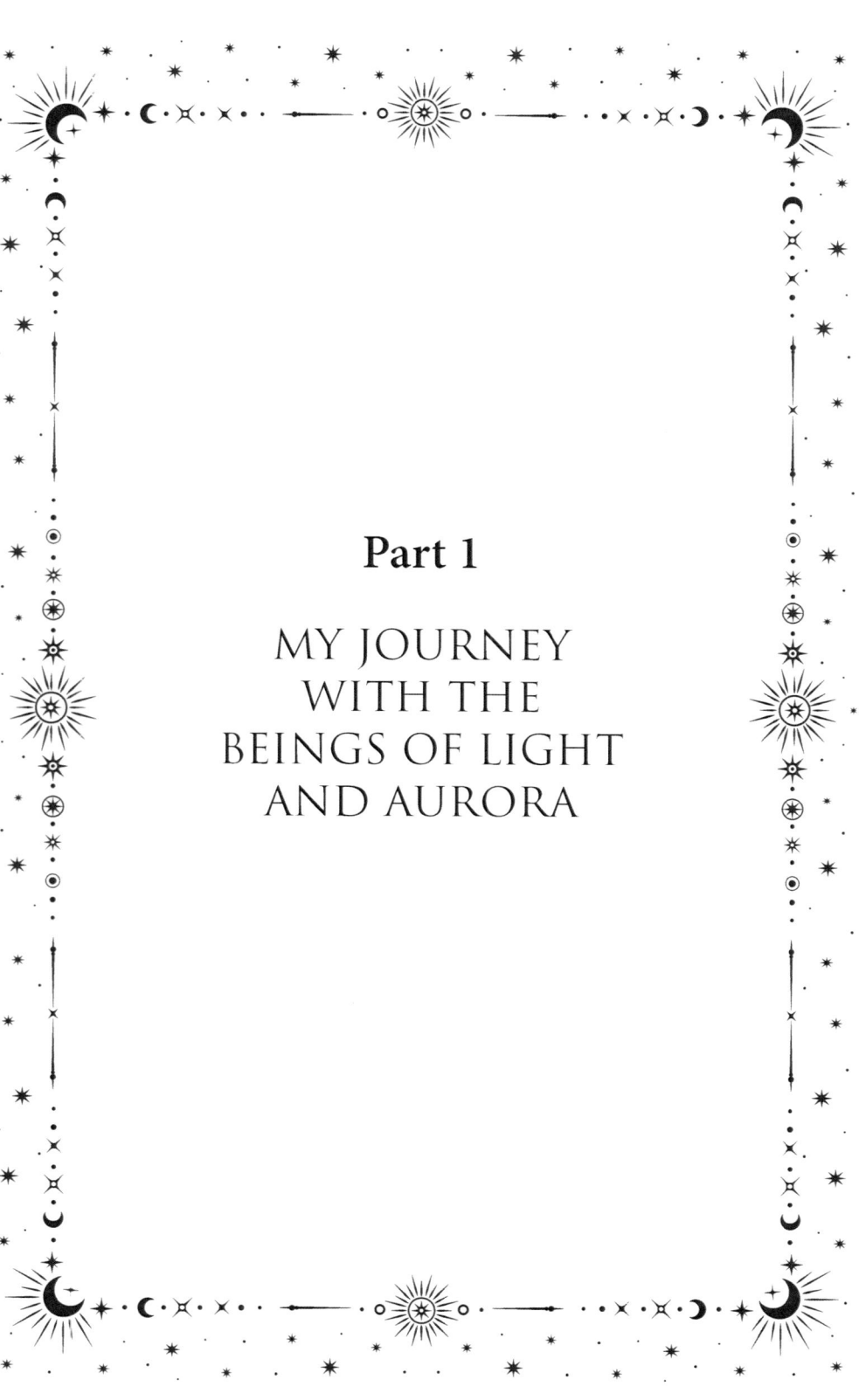

Part 1

MY JOURNEY WITH THE BEINGS OF LIGHT AND AURORA

NATURE
GIRL

Nature has always been my sanctuary. I was blessed to grow up on eighty acres of woodland forest in the magnificent Midwest. From a very young age, I spent endless hours roaming the woods amongst forest creatures under the majestic canopy of trees, wading the creeks, looking for rocks and treasures, riding horses, sleeping under the stars, and running barefoot through the fields. I spent days looking for tree fairies, knowing they were there. No matter what was happening in the world around me, I could always feel Mother Nature's warm embrace and magical energy saturating my beingness. My profound, heartfelt connection with the Earth, the trees, and Nature Spirits continued through the decades as I grew up, evolved, and went about my life.

In the early nineties, I experienced a series of traumatic events in my life that led me to a profound spiritual awakening. My dad died, my grandfather died, and my marriage died, all around the same time. My world was turned upside down. Struggling through the grief, an unexpected serendipity in 1994 led me to the Summit Lighthouse prayer line, and I began meditating daily. Little did I know I was opening a golden doorway to the higher dimensional spiritual realms. I started receiving channeled writings from the Beings of Light, a Collective of Nature Spirits, Angels, Ascended Masters, Celestial Guides, and The Great White Brotherhood (White meaning LIGHT). The emotional pain was deep, and I continued to process my grief. I remember one particularly agonizing night lying in bed, weeping and praying.

In my moment of despair, I cried out, "What is this thing that I'm in?" I continued, "I feel bigger than my body. What is life all about?"

The next morning, I felt lighter, and things began to change. As I went about my day, the word *energy* kept coming up unexpectedly. At the time, I was employed as a paralegal at a law firm specializing in toxic torts, and energy was certainly not a word I typically heard, let alone repeatedly. But it seemed that everywhere I turned, someone was using this word. After work, I briefly stopped by a bookstore to pick up a journal for my writing. As I breezed past a display aisle, I noticed two books precariously sticking out, undoubtedly beckoning me to pull them from the shelf. One book referenced the healing energy of your hands, and the other, how to read the energy of an aura. Message received! The Universe was communicating with me loud and clear, and I was listening!

Later that week, I went into a shop I frequented regularly to buy incense for my meditation practice and saw a flier for a Holistic Awareness Conference in a city nearby. I knew I had to go. During the conference, I attended an informative lecture on the Ancient Japanese Healing Art of Reiki and met my future Reiki Master-Teacher. I eagerly began my training with her, happily driving the long distance back and forth to receive my certification in the Usui Shiki Ryoho Method of Natural Healing, which would become one of the most sacred gifts of my life.

Becoming a Reiki Master-Teacher ultimately ignited my soul, opening and expanding my channel for receiving powerful, higher-dimensional life force energy. The remarkable expansion also gave me a deeper understanding of All That Is and my personal journey on this Earth.

I started a private healing arts practice in 1996, leaving the legal field and all its benefits and perks behind. *What was I doing?!* I was a single parent with a toddler, but I had to honor my truth and follow my soul's prompting like a moth to a flame.

MYSTICAL
REUNION

Life carried on. At the beginning of the new millennium, an advanced Star Being named AURORA joined the Beings of Light and myself, showing me her name wherever I went and then presenting herself to me in meditation. After her arrival, she lovingly assisted with the information brought forth in my second book, *Being Light, Beyond the Veil of The Golden Age: A Light Server's Guide to Harnessing the Energies of The New Earth,* which is offered as a spiritual Ascension tool. With AURORA's arrival, my Fleet of Light expanded. Although she was ever-present by my side, it wasn't until I experienced a critical health crisis that she began *tangibly* appearing to me.

This book and the images contained herein bridge science and spirituality like never before, opening the doorway for mankind to understand their Interconnectedness with all creatures, great and small, and all beings everywhere, as Mother Earth and her inhabitants enter The Age of Aquarius, where there is perfect peace, love, and harmony for All.

There are Benevolent Beings of Light among us, patiently waiting for our call. As humanity fans the flame of realization that we are not alone, we ignite a new template, co-creating A New Earth.

AURORA and the Beings of Light continue to work by my side as we awaken humankind, raise the planetary vibration, and build our perfected Crystalline Bodies of Light, soaring beyond the veil into The Golden Age.

WHO
HEALS
THE
HEALER

I was the healthiest person I knew. I had eaten clean for decades, was physically fit, a disciplined daily meditator since 1994, and had owned and operated my private healing arts practice for over 25 years, serving clients and students from all walks of life.

As a healer, I experienced many profound case studies over the decades—cancer reversed, tumors dissolved, blood disorders cleared, people awakening from comas after being pronounced brain dead, and spontaneous healings of all sorts. I didn't work alone. I was a channel of higher light energy and was accompanied by a beautiful fleet of Angels and Guides that assisted me. Working with thousands of clients and students from all over the world, I knew that anything could be healed and that one must visualize oneself in stellar health, bathing one's mind and spirit with positive thoughts, affirmations, and prayers. This is what I taught, believed, and wrote about.

I had been crop-dusted years earlier while running on a 98-degree day on a remote country road flanked by cornfields in the Midwest. Unbeknownst to me, the toxic chemicals lay silent in my body until making their dreadful presence known in 2013. I was told I had a rare blood disorder. Stage IV. Terminal. And that I didn't have long to live. Believing that any condition could be healed, I handled the diagnosis with hope and optimism and treated it holistically with alternative therapies for two years before synergistically integrating some Western modalities. Living a spiritual life, I knew anything was possible and kept my eyes to the light.

"You will have a miraculous healing." I kept hearing these words loud and clear.

From the very beginning, I was assured by AURORA and the Beings of Light that I would have a profound spiritual healing. No matter how horrifying it got, it was all about the *experience*, and I was to have unwavering faith. This mountain was placed before me so that I could move it and show others how to do the same. I consulted with four different doctors across the country for second, third, and fourth opinions. I was also being treated by an integrative doctor out-of-state and working closely with my local hematologist, whom I adored.

We had exhausted all the treatment modalities for the dis-ease. AURORA and the Beings of Light stayed ever-present by my side, telling me to trust, that this was all part of the process, that the healing was coming, and that I was setting a new template for humanity. I was told to call forth and anchor in the Christed Cosmic Crystalline Light I had taught and written about and direct it to the parts of my body that needed healing. I was also instructed to keep re-setting my energetic matrix and not let the medical arena imprint negative images or impressions onto my auric field.

As I continued this practice, I realized the experience was taking me to a deeper level of my soul's purpose and that I had contracted to go through this traumatic event to evolve, grow, and expand into a deeper expression of my Beingness on Earth. I was to trust with unwavering faith that I would be healed.

As my daughter and I began making the trek to a nearby university hospital, chanting affirmations and praying for a miraculous healing, we decided to look at the whole situation as an *adventure,* shifting our awareness from fear to the greater purpose and exploration that this scenario offered.

"Wow, had I really signed up for this lesson before incarnating on Earth?!" I commented.

Yes, I had, and it was imperative that I stay the course, knowing all was well.

I came close to death three times. Keeping the faith, I knew it wasn't my time and asked the doctors to be patient with my body.

The spirit of my beloved dog, Thorin, came to me several times, pleading, "PLEASE, don't give up; PLEASE, don't stop dancing."

He was loyally by my side and would be giving me undeniable signs of his presence in the coming days. He even came through in a painting by a stranger in a channeling group that mystically made its way to me.

Other deceased family members came to me as well, with encouragement and support, telling me from heaven, "You're not invited to the party."

I needed to go to the vortexes. Sedona had always been my second home. I had been making the annual pilgrimage since 1997, and it was calling my name. So off we went, my daughter and me.

The profound healing came while hiking in a favorite area of Sedona in the spring of 2018. As I communed with Nature, calling in AURORA and the Beings of Light, I could feel intense energy penetrating my crown and moving around me. As an intuitive healer and channel, I knew something spectacular and otherworldly was occurring. To our delight, my daughter and I captured magnificent images of AURORA's pastel rainbow craft in the colors of the three-fold-flame with our camera. Upon returning home, my bone marrow was clear, and I continue to thrive!

AURORA was now appearing tangibly to me. It was time for humanity to awaken and understand the higher dimensionality that is all around us. Though not always detected with the naked eye, there are Benevolent Beings of Light among us, waiting patiently for our call. This is my journey with AURORA and the Beings of Light.

THE
NEW
ERA
OF
TERRA

We are entering The Age of Aquarius and co-creating A New Earth. As we stand at the precipice of The Golden Age and journey beyond the veil into the new Era of Terra, we are asked to open our hearts and minds to the realm of all possibilities and embrace what was once only imaginable. As we do so, we ignite the ancient memory of the Infinite Beings that we are and our divine purpose on the Earth.

This book highlights and honors AURORA, a magnificent Benevolent Star Being and Collective, who have joined me and the Beings of Light in our effort to assist humanity's Awakening and Ascension into The Seventh Golden Age. AURORA is used interchangeably throughout this book as she, they, them.

AURORA and her Collective are beautiful Benevolent Star Beings that appear very humanesc, much like us. They are not just extraterrestrials; they are *Ultraterrestrials*—Higher Dimensional Light Beings, Star People, who vibrate at or above the frequency of the Angelic Realm and work primarily from the ninth through twelfth dimensions. Though they can and **do** travel in their crafts, they do not *require* them; they travel in their Light Bodies and Orbs.

AURORA comes to you as Star Fleets of Light from a Sister Galaxy, ever vigilant in their crusade to assist Planet Earth. They are here on a mission of love and peace and have chosen to be detected at this time to assist Mother Earth and her inhabitants with the Planetary Ascension and to awaken the earthlings to their Interconnectedness with All That Is. As guardians of the Earth, they encourage personal freedom through Christos Crystalline Unity Consciousness, where there is perfect peace, love, and harmony for All.

It has been my tremendous privilege to work with these Divine Celestial Beings and be a channel for their higher light knowledge. I am truly humbled by their love and illumination as we have worked together on this most sacred mission on Earth.

Preceding the Galleria portion of this book are selected *Messages to Humanity* from AURORA and her Collective. We have reached a critical point on the planet, and mankind must now awaken to the realization that We Are Not Alone. May you be filled with light and joyful anticipation as you ignite the ancient memory of Who You Are and build your perfected Body of Light!

The Beings of Light and AURORA are in full gratitude to those holding these pages and look forward to the new Era of Terra as we move more fully into The Golden Age of Light, The Age of Aquarius, and co-create A New Earth.

INTERSTELLAR MESSENGER

I have seen crafts and unidentified flying objects from a very young age. In my early 30s, the sightings began to increase dramatically. These sensational experiences have been observed from afar and up close and personal, with crafts flying slowly, silently, barely skimming the house, or gracefully gliding across the sky. Too numerous to count, the phenomena have appeared as flying saucers, plasma crafts, sparkling lights, glowing balls, and orbs on any given day.

On a beautiful fall night in 2018, a glorious full moon appeared on the horizon. As I excitedly flung open the front door to go outside and bathe in its essence with my dog Gandalf by my side, a UFO shot quickly across the sky, a prelude to the rest of the evening's events. I ran out to the front meadow, looking up at the stars, and could feel tingling all around me. Standing there, taking it in, I felt as if an electrical current was dancing around me. I stood still, knowing something tremendously transcendent was taking place.

My inner voice told me to go inside and grab my phone to take a few pictures. I resisted. I was not a person that was glued to my phone. The fewer electronic devices one had, the better. In fact, I liked being off the grid as much as possible. Still, the internal nudges continued. Not accustomed to using the camera on my phone, I continued to resist. I had just recycled my old phone, and I wasn't even sure how to fully use its replacement. As the message grew louder, I knew I had to honor the prompting, so I trotted back inside and retrieved my phone. I snapped several pictures in the dark night sky, wondering if anything would be captured. I continued my late-night stargazing, walking the property with Gandalf, until we eventually went back inside. To my delight, a myriad of images emerged as I opened my phone, with beautiful crafts and numerous orbs.

This particular evening was just one of a multitude of similar close encounters, where I have captured indescribable images of these Benevolent Ultraterrestrial Beings in their various forms and crafts. The *Interdimensional Galleria* following the *Messages to Humanity* section, features some of the most mesmerizing images of AURORA and her Interstellar Collective in their unique cosmic expression. They change form and appear as plasma crafts, flying saucers, huge pastel orbs, opalescent orbs, rainbow orbs, opaque orbs, sparkling lights, orbs that shapeshift into crafts, exquisite plasma crafts with sacred geometrical healing tools, and ethereal humanesc beings. They also sometimes appear in beautiful shades of the Aurora Borealis, or "inter-dimensional resonant tone." Though they can and **do** travel in their crafts, they do not *require* them; they travel in their Light Bodies and Orbs.

AURORA comes from a Sister Galaxy of Christos Crystalline Unity Consciousness. They are The Solar Crystal Temple Beings, Ultraterrestrials, who have answered the call to assist Mother Earth and her inhabitants with the Planetary Ascension and to re-ignite the three-fold-flame within the heart of humanity. AURORA works with the Choir of Angels beside the Cherubim and Seraphim, lovingly protecting the Golden Merkabic Throne Chariot of God. AURORA and her Collective also repair the Crystalline Planetary Grid of Light, removing negative implants, chips, machinery, and encryption from the Earth's core and human race, returning mankind to its rightful, pristine 12-strand DNA and *beyond*.

AURORA and the Beings of Light can be called upon at any time and assist All who wish to fan the flame of consciousness within and build their perfected Body of Light. Other names for the Light Body are the Crystalline Body of Light, Diamond Body, Star Body, Radiant Body, Celestial Body, Rainbow Body, Crystal Body, Resurrection Body, Spiritual Body, Christos Body, Adam Kadmon Body, or Christed Cosmic Crystalline Body of Light.

All of the photographic images in this book were taken by me or my daughter, some of which were captured with a camera while hiking, others spontaneously with a phone, and have not been edited.

I continue to have close encounters and interstellar experiences on any given day.

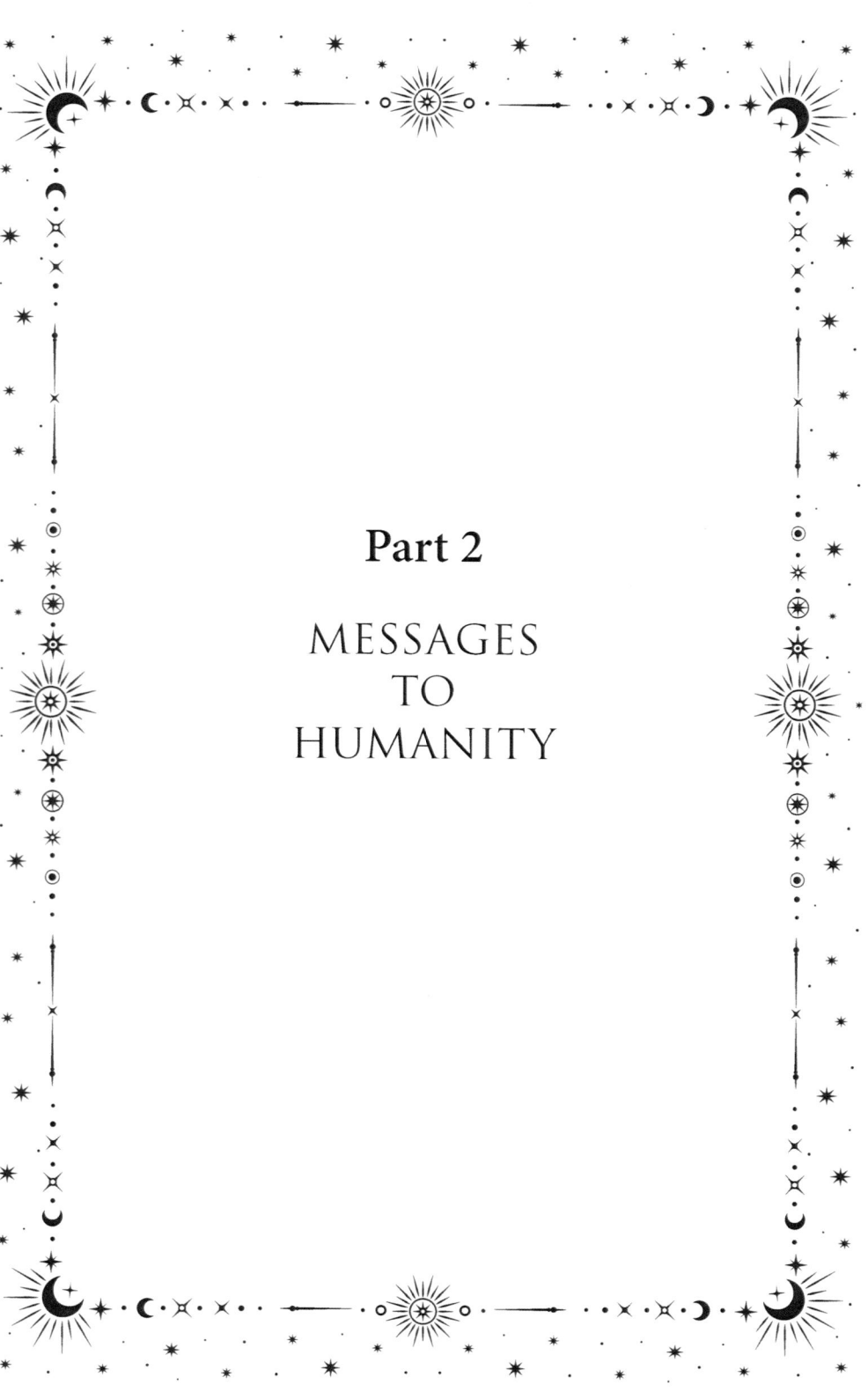

Part 2

MESSAGES
TO
HUMANITY

The following
MESSAGES TO HUMANITY
contain selected channeled excerpts from AURORA,
which she and her Collective believe are most vital to Mother Earth
and her inhabitants at this time on the planet.

The affirmations following each message
are intended to be fully absorbed, integrating and assimilating
divine KNOWINGNESS deep within your Beingness,
assisting you in your Conscious Awakening and Alchemization Process
as you raise your frequency, merge with your Merkabic Chariot,
and build your perfected
BODY OF LIGHT.

Set aside some quiet space every morning
after you arise, visualize your day unfolding in a magical way,
and DECLARE your affirmations.
Repeat each affirmation at least three times
to fully EMBODY its essence
before going on to the next.

You may also chant or sing
your affirmations, for the BEAUTY of the emotional force
assists with the deep intention of your decrees
and is delightful to the Beings in the
Celestial and Angelic Kingdoms!

GREETINGS
FROM
AURORA

I AM Aurora. I serve on the Air Fleet of The Most Radiant One, beside the Beings of Light. The Beings of Light are a Collective of Angels, Nature Spirits, Ascended Masters, Star People, and other beautiful Cosmic Guides, a Sky Branch of The Great White Brotherhood (White referring to LIGHT). I have different assignments in different dimensions, working also with the I AM Presence and violet flame teachings. I also guide the Starship of The Most Radiant One, familiarly known to you as Master Jesus or Sananda, and have taken a vow to assist in the most vital mission of guiding Planet Earth in its transition into a star.

As Aurora of Light, I come from a Sister Galaxy of Christos Crystalline Unity Consciousness, bringing you messages of Peace, Faith, and Love. I work primarily from the ninth through twelfth dimensions at the right hand of The Most Radiant One, assisting all who wish to heal, transmute, and Ascend. We serve beside Sananda as a higher-dimensional Planetary Patrol System, ever vigilant in our crusade to assist Mother Earth. We lovingly monitor your precious planet and bring forth messages of Truth, which shall set you free. From our vantage point, we see the earthlings struggling to attain the light of consciousness, negating their circumstances through self-sabotage and fear. Have faith, Children of Light, for it is your divine destiny to walk hand-in-hand in the Light of Spirit, where All is possible, as you most joyfully create the much anticipated and long-awaited Heaven on Earth and your beautiful planet evolves *beyond the veil* of The Golden Age.

COSMIC
AIRBORNE
DIVISION

Cosmic Beings of Light and Silver Chariots in the sky.

From the Cosmic Airborne Division from which we operate, we sit at the right hand of The Most Radiant One, Sananda, most familiarly known to you as Master Jesus. We are his Sky Ambassadors if you will. He encourages us to spread the message of Love, for this is the energy that can save your precious planet, which has come close to being dismantled many times at the reckless hands of man, missiles, and bombs. We are here to guide you into the new millennium and ask that you keep an open mind in the days to come, for we are kindred spirits of the earthlings, your Brothers and Sisters of Light. We are Cosmic Angels, Star People, but in a much more etheric form. We are The Solar Crystal Temple Beings, Ultraterrestrials from a Sister

Galaxy of Christos Unity Consciousness. Our energetic matrixes spin at an extreme rate, making us invisible to your physical eye. There are certain clairvoyant beings, like our beloved channel, who can detect us with the precision of their third eye or psychic eye, but in order for us to be seen by humanity, we must shift our frequency to a different caliber. This is when you see our silver chariots in the sky.

We have now chosen to be detected, for we are here to be of great service in the coming days. We will be appearing more and more in the sky to your earthling race and look forward to the day when we stand side-by-side and communicate in the Light of Spirit for the good of humanity and life on all planets throughout the Galaxies, for this is what The Golden Age has in store. Be not afraid, for we appear much like you do, quite humanesc, but shimmery, tall, thin, with fair skin and hair, we glow. We teleport and travel in our starships, crafts, orbs, and Light Bodies. We communicate from our heart centers telepathically and through our eyes. When you see us, you will feel a calming sense of peace and love, for we are Beings of Love and Light. We are ONE with you. I AM Aurora.

WHAT
IS
LIGHT
BODY

The energetic matrix that surrounds the physical vessel as it prepares to shift into its perfected light body operates at an immense speed, spinning, interacting, and intertwining with the multidimensional layers of the Universe, radiating and rippling across all space and time. This multidimensional matrix houses the codes and keys to the entire Galaxy and Universe, and the power lies within YOU to activate and ignite the ancient memory of self. THE TIME IS NOW to awaken and tap into this infinite sea of knowledge, to at last merge with the Cosmic Pillar of Divine Light, to expand and reveal your true spiritual identity, your Divine Blueprint, your *Essence,* your calling.

The cells and subatomic molecular structure of the human vessel hold the supreme intelligence of All That Is. As you nourish and fill your cells with light, you ignite the ancient memory that is encapsulated throughout your Beingness. As you consciously work to build your Body of Light, you raise your frequency, allowing your soul to communicate with the cells in all living things around you. As you share your light with others, you increase the vibration of the planet; you become a precious link in the Great Shift.

Light is the most vital source on the planet, and when you fill your vessel with LIGHT, you begin your activation process, restructuring, recalibrating, and recoding your energetic matrix back to its original framework. You begin the process of shifting into your perfected LIGHT BODY.

I AM Aurora.

AFFIRMATION

I AM flooding my body with
Christed Cosmic Crystalline Light.

I AM living in my
perfected Light Body now.

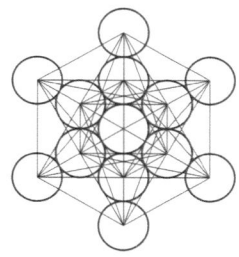

CHRISTED
COSMIC
CRYSTALLINE
BODY
OF
LIGHT

As you evolve spiritually and drop density, you move into a higher vibrational body that enables you to explore other dimensional realities.

The multidimensional matrix that houses your physical body continues to evolve and prepare you for your emergence into the Light and acceleration into The Golden Age. As your light body upgrades and prepares, it vibrates into a spinning vortex that houses all the molecules and subparticles containing the codes and keys to Nature and All That Is. As you bring more light into your body, you activate higher light frequencies, recoding, reconnecting, and reactivating your DNA back to its original 12-strand state of being and BEYOND. As you fill your vessel with light, you help reinforce the Crystalline Planetary Network of Light and assist in the mass awakening of humanity.

The multi-crystalline structure of the human energy field contains trillions of atoms and particles, vibrating at the speed of light, inviting you to merge with your light body. The technographics of the evolved light body allow you to explore other dimensional realities through astral travel and teleportation, for this is the way of the future in the new Era of Terra. Your body will be your personal *craft* and as you think of a desired geographical destination, you will be instantaneously transported there. This is possible because as you transcend linear time, you raise your vibration to exist in a higher dimensional state of being, which allows you to easily manifest your expansive vision and destination of choice. You will have the ability to travel through many portals of energy with magnificent colors, petals, tones, and landscapes.

Some have asked what will happen to electronics as The Golden Age continues to expand and emerge. Earthlings are caught up in the technological age of electronics and instant gratification, if you will. As Light Beings, you will house your own inner navigation system, so to speak. As you fully merge with the spherical energies of The Golden Age and evolve into the multidimensional being that you came here to be, you will be less interested in such *gadgets.*

Your body will be your chariot. You will have everything you need within your Beingness, for you will be operating from your Heart Centers, which are infinitely faceted. You will be speaking with mental telepathy. You will be transporting yourself, teleporting, in your own personal craft, which is YOU.

The demographics of the dark side have encouraged human beings to be distracted from Nature and have placed a candy store of electronics at your disposal to keep you separate from God, Source, All That Is.

We ask, have you ever really allowed yourself to spend the day in Nature and bask in the energies of the Divine, which emanates from the trees, the ocean, the hills, the mountains, the rocks, the streams?

For those of you who have, you know the feeling that permeates your Beingness. You feel the presence and ONENESS, the calm, the centeredness that Nature offers.

Nature was created by Source to hold the codes and keys to the awakening soul, to nourish and heal you. So, encourage your loved ones, your children, your kin to go outside and spend time with the Nature Spirits and the Elementals, for they, too, are the Guardians of the Earth and have much to teach you. Spend time communing with the great willow, the oak, the flowers, and velvety moss, for they contain vast information and knowledge waiting to be explored. Feel the tingling vibration of light streaming through the trees as it speaks to you, for this is all part of your soul's education and evolution into higher light form.

The goal on Planet Earth at this time is to fully realize your God Self, to become ONE with the I AM Presence, Source, the Spark of Divinity in each and every one of you. To raise the vibration of humanity to a level of exalted spiritual comprehension, allowing you to merge with spherical time and space, to Ascend. As you fill your body with light, you raise your frequency, preparing you for this flight.

I AM Aurora.

AFFIRMATION

I AM one with my Higher Self, my I AM Presence within.

I AM vibrating in my highest frequency
and merging with my perfected Light Body now.

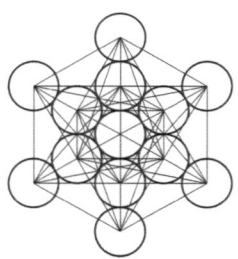

THE
MAGIC
OF
NATURE

As you spend time in NATURE, you respond to an inner coding, creating a high vibrational current that aligns you with your true Remembrance of Self and deeper understanding of All That Is, for Nature holds the keys to higher light knowledge.

The philharmonics of the body's energetic matrix are closely connected to Nature's rhythm. As you cradle yourself in the arms of Nature, you receive divine downloads that support your mission and journey on this plane. As you embrace the crown glory of Nature, a whole new tapestry presents, assisting you in resolving any questions or perplexities that may have eluded you for years, decades, or even lifetimes. As you forge the trail of higher consciousness, opening up to Mother Earth and communicating your global vision for humanity and your soul's evolution, your path is lit, for Nature holds the keys to the gateway of higher cosmic knowledge. As you spend time in Nature and bless and respect the Earth, you receive coded filaments, which ignite, awaken, and support your journey on this plane.

Dear Ones, we would ask that you live in harmony with Nature each and every day, for every living thing on the planet has a purpose in the divine plan and reflects back to you all you need to see, supplying you with crucial guidance.

We ask, have you ever really stopped to look at the Beauty of Nature and seen yourself in the Eyes of God?

Have you ever really listened to the sweet hum of spring peepers and cicadas, only to be elevated to a trance-like state, catapulted into what feels like a higher dimensional parallel reality?

This is because the essence of Nature touches the deepest aspect of your original core blueprint, back to the beginning of time before your flame was separate from Source.

Mother Nature knows when you adorn her precious ground, she patiently awaits your arrival and delivers vital information to you through your feelings, emotions, creative insights, and downloads. The flowers have messages for you, the birds, the bees, the trees, and more. As you see the Spark of God in ALL living things, you awaken to the higher dimensional reality of who you are, and your soul emerges, shining light and awakening others. Accept her invitation to kick off your shoes, sit amongst the flowers and moss, walk the woods, wade the streams, meditate against a tree, bathe in the sea.

Through your energetic connection with the Earth, you set *templates* to anchor in higher light form. As you do so, you strengthen the Planetary Bridge and Crystalline Cosmic Grid, becoming a precious link in the Ascension process of the planet. Even the most subtle, tender act of walking barefoot on the Earth and really feeling the sand and grass beneath your feet is an act of merging with the Divine.

Can you not feel the presence of God permeate every cell of your Being through your state of centeredness, peace, and calm when you merge with the splendid energy of the trees, the earth, the mountains, streams, meadows, and vast seas? For Mother Earth's aura is expansive and forms an energetic matrix, encapsulating you in the sacredness of her womb.

I AM Aurora.

AFFIRMATION

I AM receiving my Spirit-sanctioned infusions,
downloads and mission directives now.

I AM one with Nature and All of God's Creatures.

THE
HEALING
POWER
OF
LIGHT

LIGHT is a living consciousness and transforms any challenging situation. The more LIGHT you bring into your body, the higher the frequency. The higher the frequency, the closer you are to God, your Buddha Nature, All That Is. Build your Body of Light.

LIGHT is a miraculous source of healing, and as you pull more light into your body, you oxygenate your nervous system, accelerating your physical healing and soul's evolution on Earth. We ask you now to remember that you are Light Beings and that any areas of unease in the physical vessel can be healed with light. Call forth CRYSTALLINE Light to the areas of the body that are vying for your attention. Flood every single cell of your vessel with this crystalline light and ask that the light be directed to any areas of pain or *dis-ease,* for every cell in your body holds intelligence and responds to your divine directive. You have this ability as a Child of God, Source Energy.

Step outside in the beauty of nature and gaze up to the sky; focus on the rays of light as they enter your third eye center, pineal gland, crown chakra, heart, and every pore of your Being. Invite the rays of crystalline diamond light to heal, transform, and awaken you to the exquisite Multidimensional Being you came here to be. As you do so, you activate latent ancient coding and memories stored deep within your consciousness, assisting you with your realignment and healing process. Then give thanks!

Pure LIGHT is your soul's natural state of locomotion and expression, so we ask that you allow yourself to bask in the luminous reflection of your divine essence and shower this light upon all you meet. As you answer the call of your internal song, honoring the truth and light within your heart, you illuminate those souls waiting to awaken.

And so it is, I AM Aurora.

AFFIRMATION

I AM a temple of God's miraculous healing light.

I AM in supreme and stellar health.
Every single cell of my body is radiating in divine perfection now.

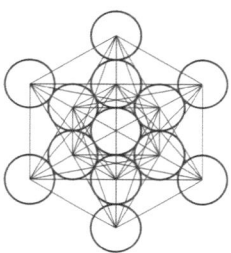

TEMPLE
OF
TRANSPORT

Honor and respect your physical body, for it has a consciousness of its own and has served as your faithful Port of Call through your incarnation on this plane.

Your physical body is a gift from Creator, and you have chosen your particular, unique embodiment to assist you through your navigation on Earth. Some earthlings have mistreated their bodies of flesh because they believe they are separate from Source and that they are not connected. Your body is your TEMPLE OF TRANSPORT, and you must treat it with the utmost respect and honor. You are housing the exquisite multidimensional matrix that is YOU, and your physical vessel has been through much as you have been educated in the Laws of Spirit.

Honor, nourish, and replenish your Body Temple, and it will bring you great results in return. Fill your body with light and love. Spend time in nature, bask in the glory of things that make your heart sing. Commune with your physical vessel as if you were talking to a faithful friend. Look at your reflection in the mirror daily and tell yourself you are very loved. Thank your body for housing and carrying you through your most sacred journey on this planet, for it has been your Temple of Transport, your faithful *Port of Call* on Earth.

I AM Aurora.

AFFIRMATION

I AM grateful for my faithful Port of Call.

I AM honoring and nourishing my Temple of Transport now.

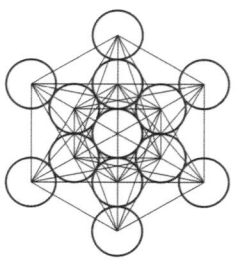

PERFECTED
LIGHT
BODY

As you anchor in higher light energies, you build your Body of Light, activating dormant codes, keys, and filaments within, igniting a deeper understanding of your soul's purpose and remembrance of the Radiant Being that you are.

As you evolve spiritually, your Body of Light GLOWS and vibrates at a sensational velocity, radiating luminous light to those around you. This multi-crystalline structure of the human energy field contains trillions of atoms and particles vibrating at the speed of light, inviting you to merge with your Light Body.

Your perfected Crystalline Light Body is immense, and as you begin to merge with the multidimensional geometrical sphere around you, the atoms, molecules, and subparticles begin to spin, activating your soul's merkaba to manufacture the speed you need to evolve into your highest dimensional state. This spinning vortex is your Celestial Throne Chariot and is capable of transporting you across time and space to anywhere your soul desires. It allows you to bilocate to various places in time simultaneously.

For now, you must work on maximizing your light quotient and holding this divine frequency so that you will be prepared when the time is near. Fill your body, mind, and Spirit with loving thoughts and light, live mindfully, and nurture your Merkabic Chariot, for soon, you will be operating in your higher dimensional vehicle of choice.

I AM Aurora, and I bring you this message today.

AFFIRMATION

I AM maximizing my light quotient now.

I AM beautifully merged
with my Celestial Throne Chariot now.

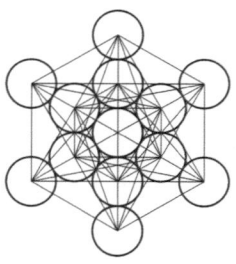

YOUR
HEART
IS THE
PORTAL OF
HIGHER
LIGHT
FREQUENCY

The Light of your Heart is the GATEWAY through which your Higher Self communicates. Let the Compass of your Heart guide you.

We speak of the multifaceted jewel of the heart, for it is through this heart center that you shall operate in the new Era of Terra. This magnificent diamond crystalline structure houses the codes and keys to your higher consciousness and fully awakened multidimensional self, each intricate facet layered with the infinite knowledge of each soul's unique AWAKENING to the light of Spirit and evolution on Earth.

The multifaceted jewel of the heart is nestled deep within the Secret Chamber of the Heart, where the three-fold-flame resides inside each and every one of you. As you take the vow to *re-ignite* the ancient memory of who you are, the holographic matrix within the diamond heart is activated, showering spheres of incandescent light across all space and time, healing and transmuting yourselves and the planet.

As you breathe in and feel the golden liquid light within your heart GLOW, you raise your vibration, igniting this multifaceted matrix to expand through the Secret Chamber of your Heart, radiating unconditional love to all you meet. As you activate this *portal* of higher light knowledge, you place yourself in the direct flow of the cosmic language of light, and your path is lit, for your *Heart* is the seat of wisdom and intuition, your divine connection to Source through the body temple.

So, Dear Ones, we ask that you honor and nourish your heart. Return to the sacred and make each day an offering. Speak, act, and operate from the highest place within your beingness, for the way of the HEART is the way of the future in the new Era of Terra after Mother Earth has made her grand alignment.

As you open the doorway of your bejeweled heart, you fan the glowing embers of the three-fold-flame within, for through this doorway of stillness resides the KNOWINGNESS that you are ONE with All That Is.

So, we ask that you turn the key, unlock your heart, step inside, and roam the vast, beautiful wilderness of your magnificent soul. Your hearts will sing with the bright light of Spirit, and you will adorn sparkling crowns of glory on your heads, for your spiritual centers associated with your psychic vision and cosmic wisdom will be fully activated, glowing, and operating like a well-lit craft.

The first step is to master the *Compass of the Heart*, for your HEART is the portal of higher knowledge, your guiding light and navigator.

We love you and salute you always. I AM Aurora.

AFFIRMATION

I AM allowing the Compass of my Heart
to guide me always.

I AM opening the Secret Chamber of my Heart
and fanning the glowing embers
of the three-fold-flame within.

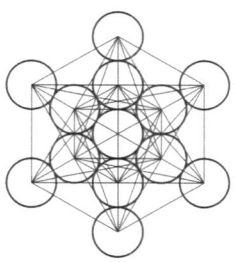

INTEGRATING COSMIC STREAMS OF LIGHT

As you embrace the new waves of crystalline light showering the planet, you ignite higher dimensional coding, reconnecting and reactivating your DNA back to its original framework of 12-strand and Beyond.

As solar flares and eclipses continue to increase and bombard the Earth with stepped-up velocity, your human vessel may experience an increased sensation of spinning or vertigo. This is because the solar flares and increased infusions of cosmic energy showering the planet cause your Merkabic Chariot, the exterior sacred geometrical energetic matrix that surrounds your physical body, to spin at an increased rate.

An affirmation that is helpful at this time is "I AM integrating and assimilating these high vibrational frequencies now!"

We would ask that you spend additional time in NATURE during the increased solar activity and walk the Earth, preferably with the bare soles of your feet, for this will assist you in grounding in these powerful waves of light. You may also find it beneficial to meditate against a tree, lay on the earth, or spend extra time in your flower or vegetable gardens. Many highly sensitive Starseeds and Light Servers walk a labyrinth as a focused intention for anchoring in these sometimes challenging streams of energy.

For some of you, you may need to fully merge with these energies before going into a horizontal position at times of rest. Simply stating, "I AM beautifully merged with these high vibrational frequencies now," will assist you and lessen the spinning effect.

Frankincense oil and myrrh are also very beneficial for grounding in the new spherical energies. We honor you for your diligent effort in integrating these sensational frequencies, for when you EMBODY the waves of light showering the Earth, you become a precious link in the transformation of the planet. You build your Crystalline Body of Light and strengthen the Planetary Grid.

I AM Aurora, and I serve you from my heart center, blessing each and every one of you today.

AFFIRMATION

I AM embodying the crystalline waves of light
showering the Earth.

I AM fully aligned
with my Merkabic Chariot now.

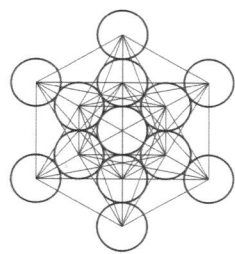

BRINGERS
OF
LIGHT

You are a MAJESTIC Ray of Light. Release the illusional chains that bind you and allow your magnificent Spirit to SOAR!

How do we measure the concept of time? What molecules and subparticles bond together to place us exactly where we are at any given time, including but not limited to parallel lives?

You chose to be here in this particular lifetime to hold the frequency of light, to fully embody the vibration of love, and to re-ignite your Body of Light, for you are the Way Showers, ushering your planet into The Golden Age. You wonder what your role is, what your part in the play is. We are here to tell you that as you walk the Earth, you set energetic templates that serve as *portals* to higher dimensional light energy. In this way, the waves of light that shower the planet, as well as solar flares, eclipses, and other energies associated with astrological alignments, can easily be anchored in and grounded.

Those of you reading these pages have come here to serve as Ambassadors or BRINGERS OF LIGHT, if you will. Wherever you go, whatever you do, you radiate your light and set energetic templates to assist in transforming places on the planet.

There may have been times in your life when you wondered, "Where am I, and what am I doing here?"

You may have taken what was perceived to be a wrong turn, inadvertently gone around the same block several times, or were drawn to travel to a certain geographical location that may have left you feeling daunted. However, you were always guided and protected, and in your wanderings, you were not lost. Each of you reading these pages chose to come here at this particular time to embody Christos Crystalline Light, to move more fully into the frequency of LOVE, and to usher humanity into UNITY Consciousness.

There are some of you who have wondered why you were placed in the particular Earth families you are in. When you were younger, some of you may have experienced abuse or were extremely misunderstood by siblings or parents. You may look unlike any of your kin. And, though you were surrounded by many acquaintances growing up, you may have chosen to have just one or two close friends—confidantes, if you will. You were perhaps a loner and felt homesick for something that you couldn't quite place your finger on or assimilate. Some of you may have had traumatic experiences in your adult life that have led you to a deeper understanding and awakening.

All of these circumstances, some tragic and treacherous as they have been, served to evolve you into your highest potential. To search for the meaning of LIGHT and to bring light to those around you, for you were placed exactly where you needed to be to transform, heal, and recalibrate the energy of others. To access the ability to understand, serve, and counsel other earthlings more fully, for you are Majestic Beings of Light placed on *Assignment* on Earth. Ignite your divine blueprint and awaken to your grand and splendid purpose on this plane.

I AM Aurora and I bring you these messages today. I AM here to assist you in awakening and carrying forth the Violet Flame of Spiritual Knowledge through the remembrance of self and the eminence of light.

AFFIRMATION

I AM a BRINGER OF LIGHT,
remembering the role I AM here to fulfill.

I AM igniting and living my Divine Blueprint,
my grand and splendid purpose on this Earth.

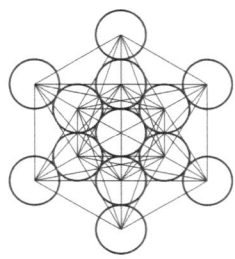

YOUR
BODIES
AS
PERSONAL
CRAFTS

You were born to SHIMMER. As you call forth and anchor in higher light frequency, you build your Crystalline Body of Light.

Your physical vessel holds an immense amount of light, and as you cross the energetic veil into The Golden Age, you will be navigating in your maximized light body, for it is through this vessel you shall travel. In the years to come, your body will serve as your personal craft, teleporting you to any geographical destination of choice. Your vessel is capable of holding an enormous amount of light, for this is what builds and amps up your perfected light body. Like the fuel for a car, your body will require LIGHT. So, every day, in every way, fill your vessel with light.

Simply state, "I AM flooding my body with Christed Cosmic Crystalline Light now."

Radiate this energy to all you meet, for when you share your light and love with others, your physical temple replenishes and GLOWS. As you continue to *recycle* this high-velocity light energy, an immense effervescent crystalline frequency emanates from the multifaceted jewel of the heart.

We would ask that you spend time out of doors in the natural sunlight and allow yourself to bask in the energy of Mother Earth, for this, too, fills your body with light. Other ways to fuel your light body are acts of loving kindness, meditation, singing, chanting, laughing, loving, and spending time in NATURE. Walk, hike, and lay on the earth with bare feet and skin. Cleanse your systems daily with fruits, vegetables, and mineral baths. Eat clean, pure, live foods and drink plenty of clear spring water. Lovingly bless your meals before consuming them.

View and immerse yourself in Sacred Geometry. *Return to the Sacred* and make your home your spiritual altar, filled with inspirational art, Mother Earth's beautiful bounty, and things that bring you joy. Flood your mind, body, and spirit with positive thoughts, words, affirmations, and prayers throughout the day, as these cleanse, rewire, and reprogram the cells of your beingness.

Weed your *Spiritual Garden* and let go of any activities or energies that no longer serve your highest good. What we are speaking of, Beloveds, are low-vibrational negative thoughtforms, patterns, individuals, environments, electronics, and media, to name a few.

Protect your energetic matrixes and vortexes by planting trees around the outside or border perimeters of your personal properties, as this is one of the few ways to mitigate the negative and damaging electromagnetic surges which stream from adjoining homes, land, and nearby structures.

Surround yourselves with White Light daily, with an overlay of Archangel Michael's Golden Armor of Light, for this, too, shall keep your energetic bodies protected and vibrating at a high velocity.

And always remember, Dear Ones, that negative energies, words, judgment, anger, and rage lower one's frequency and fragment the energy field. This can cause short circuitry within the physical vessel and Throne Chariot or Merkabic field. When this occurs, one will feel uncentered, depressed, angry, or anxious.

One of the quickest ways to recalibrate your system is to bathe yourself with sacred affirmations, chants, songs, and prayers, for this will reset your energetic matrix and rewire your cells. Spending time in NATURE, forest bathing, and utilizing the powerful benefits of Mother Earth's healing minerals, herbs, oils, and crystals will also recalibrate your energy field.

In doing these things, you will hasten your acceleration process on a vaster level, maximizing your light quotient as you build your Body of Light.

I AM Aurora.

AFFIRMATION

I AM calling forth and anchoring in
crystalline diamond light codes now.

I AM glowing in inner illumination!

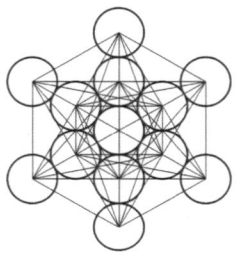

LINEAR
TIME
A THING
OF THE
PAST

As you TRANSCEND linear time, you exist in a higher dimensional state of being, which allows you to easily access your destination of choice. You will have the ability to travel through many portals of energy with magnificent colors, petals, tones, and landscapes. As you integrate these new spherical crystalline energies showering the Earth, your multidimensional faculties expand. You become ONE with your Body of Light.

The essence of time is an interesting thing, is it not, for as you begin to shift into your perfected light body, you start to lose track of linear reality as you know it. At this juncture on your planet, you are in an in-between state of being. One minute, you may feel like things are progressing so rapidly that it's difficult to keep up. Random spurts of ecstatic bliss and joy may occur within your beingness. Yet, in the next moment, you may feel you have entered a time warp in space where everything seems to slow down, as if you have pierced an inter-dimensional bubble and are in an ethereal holding pattern of sorts. This is because, at this point in time, you are straddling the energies of both realities, and you feel *suspended.*

In the days ahead, it will become clearer that you have bridged the gap, so to speak, as you continue to upgrade your Body of Light and traverse to and from the expanded realms. As you ride these elevated waves of crystalline energy, you will experience more and more joy, peace, and love in your surroundings and reality and spend less time nurturing lower vibrational stories.

As you transcend linear time, you raise your vibrational stature and exist in a stepped-up frequency, which allows you to more easily manifest your highest vision of self and the ultimate vision for mankind globally. As you trust the insights you receive, you broaden the portal of cosmic knowledge and become a *Conductor* of this new spherical energy. The heartbeat of your multidimensional soul quickens and glows as you lovingly embrace the remembrance of self and your planetary role!

For now, we ask you to keep building your Body of Light and know that we are by your side, lifting you up in all that you do.

I AM Aurora.

AFFIRMATION

I AM living in spherical time now.

I AM a Divine CONDUCTOR,
a conscious co-creator
of The New Earth.

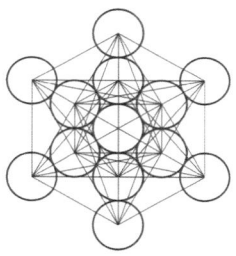

EARTHLY
ANGELS
AMONG
US

You are an INTERSTELLAR Traveler, here on Assignment to assist humanity's awakening and transition into The Golden Age of Light.

There are members of our Sky Borne Division who are walking the Earth that look much like you, for they are specialists in assisting planets ascend. These earthly angels, some of whom are reading these pages, are helping mankind and the planet raise its consciousness and prepare for Ascension. These are the calm, patient, compassionate beings that commonly work in the healing, writing, music, and creative fields, though they are from all walks of life. They are the Star Travelers of the planet. Some are not fully awakened to the realization that they are from a higher dimensional plane of existence but will be attuned to this knowledge soon.

For those who are aware, you can recognize them by a glow in their eyes, a peace in their hearts, a presence in their countenance. They love nature and animals. Compassion is their battle cry. These are souls, like our cherished channel, and some of you holding these pages, who have returned to Earth from other star systems during the Ascension process to assist in the mass awakening of humanity. Some come from the Order of Christos, returning from the Gnostic and Essene lines, faithful members of the Allegiance of Light. Others come from different star systems, also intrinsically connected with the Law of One, or Unity Consciousness.

They have taught, guided, and led the masses to bask in the frequency of Light, Self-Realization, and Unity Intelligence, many for centuries. They carry the Torch of Freedom, bringing forth the principles of the I AM Presence, personal sovereignty, and Unity Consciousness, for when one REMEMBERS they are not separate from God, Spirit, Source, they are bathed in the knowingness that all is possible, and they merge with the multifaceted crystalline jewel of the heart.

I AM Aurora, I honor you deeply and greatly support you in your Remembrance of Self and divine duty on the Earth.

AFFIRMATION

I AM an Interstellar Traveler,
activating my assignment
of duty on this Earth.

I AM a Guardian of Light,
carrying the Torch of FREEDOM
for humanity to awaken!

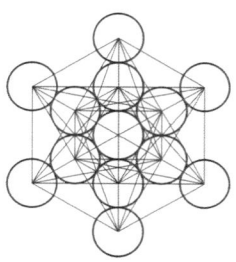

GALACTIC
STAR
FAMILY

Your Star Family of Light is around you, assisting with the planetary shift, anxiously awaiting your joyful reunion.

Your Galactic Family of Light has not forgotten you; in fact, we are in your very presence. We radiate with pride at all that you have done to REMEMBER who you are and step into your soul's mission on this plane, in preparation for the coming Age of Light. We communicate with you through feelings of loving energy, thoughts, creative insights, downloads, and inspired moments, but most of all, in your times of stillness. We hear your cries of concern and despair; we feel your joy and laughter.

KNOW that we surround you in love, holding you in the highest esteem, for you have chosen to be an active member of the

Unified Division of Light, holding the frequency for the much-anticipated Heaven on Earth.

We come to you as Star Fleets of Light, ever vigilant in our crusade to save your most precious Planet Earth. We have been by your side through the ages, but you have not seen us. We walk beside you and fill your atmosphere with our sacred starships to patrol and protect you, for we are your Star Families of Light. We serve beside Sananda, The Most Radiant One, in our mission of Peace on Earth. ·

In days to come, you will see us, and what a joyful occasion it will be, for we have long awaited our connection in Spirit, to walk hand-in-hand with you, our beloved Brothers and Sisters of Light, to live in peace and harmony in a world filled with love, unity, and the divine glory of Spirit. The Heaven on Earth you have anticipated will make manifest, and you will be astounded by the Beauty of Nature and the camaraderie of ALL life on the planet, for you will be ONE with All That Is!

You have chosen the side of Light, and for that, we applaud you greatly. The dark forces will soon be completely diminished from your planet, and your DNA will be restored to its rightful, once pristine 12-strand and beyond as you navigate in your perfected light bodies, your multidimensional Crystalline Throne Chariots.

Some of you have asked how you will know your Star Families when they arrive. We would like to tell you that we are already with you. We are of a high vibrational energy that emanates love, compassion, and light. You will feel our love in your heart centers. You will have the sense that you are ONE with us and you may feel overwhelmed with emotion and weep, for your soul has long awaited our arrival.

As previously stated through our channel, we appear very humanesc, but more ethereal, shimmery; we glow. We may also appear as ORBS, which are floating, translucent spheres of light in different shapes and forms. We are fair-skinned with fair hair and normally wear long flowing robes, but are sometimes in our galactic aviator apparel, which appears as a uniform with glowing emblems. Our palms radiate a violet light, which is the violet flame of Spirit.

We will communicate with you through our heart centers, which will emanate a bright light. You will also notice a bright light that radiates from our pineal gland or third-eye center of telepathic communication. We will speak to you as well through telepathy and our eyes. It will be a reunion of utmost joy and supreme remembrance.

We hold the field for the coming days as you prepare for this disclosure, when your government officials take their needed steps so that we may decloak our starships, and you may acknowledge us living and walking beside you. Until then, know that we surround you and embrace you always.

In joyful anticipation and devotion, I AM Aurora.

AFFIRMATION

I AM seeing and communicating clearly
with my Star Family of Light.

I AM a Majestic Being of Light
living in my Ascendancy now.

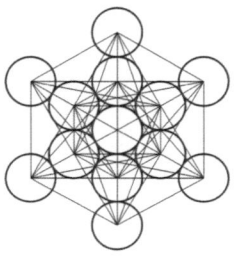

IMAGINATION

Your IMAGINATION is the canvas through which you create your Reality.

Beloveds, we ask that you allow yourselves to bask in the childlike wonder and imagination of visualizing every area of your life exactly the way you wish it to be, for your *Imagination* is the canvas through which you create your Reality.

We ask that you not dwell on things that you do *not* wish to experience, but instead on what you would like to ATTAIN and move toward it gallantly, as if you have already achieved it. Let your cup runneth over with beautiful dreams and ideals, and do not be dismayed by the reactions or responses of others, for through your vision and steadfast faith, you shall manifest your desires and be a Guidepost to many.

The Spark of God within you, Source, All That Is, ignites your imagination and serves as the golden key. When you truly believe within your heart, with unwavering faith, with absolute KNOWINGNESS, then *Anything* is possible. For Knowingness is the step beyond Believing.

As you begin to see yourself as the magnificent, majestic, multidimensional soul that you are, empowered and fully capable of being all that you came here to be, you emanate the luminous light of Spirit. You claim your birthright as a co-creator and become a precious link in strengthening the Crystalline Planetary Grid.

So, Beloveds, hold fast to the enchantment within your hearts, to all that is lovely and true to you, for through your unwavering perseverance, all that you envision shall be yours by divine right. Bask in the energy of FAITH. Be still and KNOW that you are God, a Divine Alchemist.

I AM Aurora.

AFFIRMATION

I AM the embodiment of Childlike Wonder!

I AM joyfully basking
in my IMAGINATION, through which I create my reality.

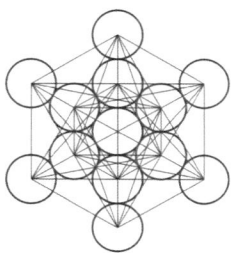

RELIGION, POLITICS, AND MANIPULATION OF THE SACRED BOOK

The TRUTH shall set you free!

Beloveds, how dear you are, for you have steadfastly continued your journeys into the Light through the mist of clouded and misperceived notions of the dark forces. You have stayed true to yourselves through the light of Source, and your reward is coming as you merge with the Cosmic Pillar of Crystalline Light and become one with your true multidimensional selves.

Dear Ones, keep your eyes to the light always, for when you choose love, peace, and equality, you are ONE with Creator, Source, All That Is. Religion and politics have been misconstrued and misrepresented by the dark forces to invoke panic amongst the earthlings, in hopes of controlling the masses through fear, shame, and guilt. Spirit would never do such things to the Allegiance of Light Servers, for Source knows your roles on the planet and honors and cherishes every one of you reading these pages.

The Illuminati and other dark forces have attempted to misinterpret your mystical teachings of long ago and remold the sacred book into something it is not, through blatant revision and deletion of material in gigantic proportion, in order to impose fear and wreak havoc on the Earth. We thank you for holding the torch of light within your hearts. We know the journey has not been easy and we honor and pledge ourselves to your faithfulness in service, to walking the path, for we have reached a time when the final strands of the dark ones are leaving.

The LIGHT has prevailed, and soon, you will be free to walk hand-in-hand in the Light of Spirit with all living creatures in the frequency of peace, love, and harmony for ALL.

In faithful service, I AM Aurora.

AFFIRMATION

I AM a faithful servant of the LIGHT.

I AM a vessel of Divine Truth and Wisdom.

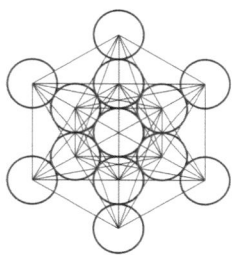

POWER POINTS ON THE PLANET

When you explore the multidimensional doorways available to you, you activate ancient cellular memories, and a deeper remembrance of self emerges.

There are numerous power spots all over the world where crafts enter and exit through portals. Some of you have power points or vortexes on your personal properties where your Star Families of Light enter and exit from time to time, downloading and teaching you what you need to know at different intervals throughout the day. Other power spots include areas in Sedona, Mt. Shasta, New Mexico, Tibet, Peru, Egypt, India, the Yucatan, Africa, Estes Park, Stonehenge, and the Midwest, to name a few.

As people frequent these areas, they receive downloads and infusions of light, which amplify and code their energy fields, upgrading and recalibrating their energetic matrixes to a level that is needed for their soul's evolution and integration into their light bodies. Each soul will be drawn to the area that best suits their merkabic needs for upgrading and realignment. We would ask that you allow yourself to travel to areas of inner prompting without second-guessing yourselves so that you will progress in the manner your soul intended.

Many individuals who do healing and creative work have chosen to live in vortex areas of sacred vibration, as it enhances the energies of their work and communication with the Higher Dimensional Beings that accompany them. In addition, many Starseeds have been drawn to live on land that has been frequented by UFOs or that has housed crop circles, as this is another means of communication with their Star Families of Light.

This is very important to those of you who are Starseeds that are fulfilling your missions, as you are accompanied by crafts at your place of domain or residence—whether you consciously see them or not—to continually support, heal, and guide you, especially in times of rest and sleep. Some of you have been prompted to live in the natural countryside or outskirts of town, as Nature is vital in your evolution, faithfully assisting you as you hold the frequency for the planet.

In divine adoration, we are the Beings of Light and Aurora.

AFFIRMATION

I AM calling forth and anchoring in
my Ascension light codes now!

I AM integrating, assimilating, and sustaining
my divine downloads, infusions, and mission directives!

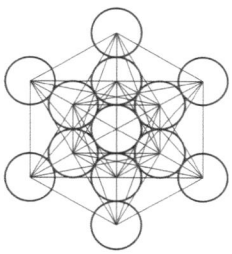

LOVE
IS
THE
ANSWER

As humanity ignites the Flame of Realization that we are ONE, the Cosmic Bridge is strengthened, for where you are, I AM.

LOVE is the most powerful force throughout the Galaxies, and what we would like to tell you is that through LOVE, the Earth will make its shift into its grand alignment in the stars. Through LOVE, all things will be healed, and through LOVE, you shall save your beautiful planet, and the history of the Cosmos will be rewritten forevermore. Love is transformational and flows through the deepest recesses of your Beingness. Love dissolves all separateness.

We ask that you not waste time fighting over dogmatic or political issues, Dear Ones. It matters not what your religion or affiliation of choice is, for when the Trinity of *Creator Energy* is formed with the *Intention* and *Good of All*, the Spark of Divinity is ignited in the hearts of all mankind. Where there is Peace, there is LOVE, and where there is Tolerance and Equality, allowing all people to be who they are, there is UNITY.

We ask that you feel the love within your hearts, for it is through this portal that your luminosity and Ascension begins. The precious, multifaceted jewel within the Secret Chamber of your Heart has waited many lifetimes to fully merge with the Light of Spirit, to commune with the I AM Presence, to at last become ONE with the three-fold-flame of consciousness.

Your HEART is the PORTAL through which your Higher Self communicates, and nothing less than LOVE will exist in the higher-dimensional energies that will bathe your planet in its refurbished state of Christos Unity Consciousness. Nature has attempted to share this sacred knowledge with mankind through the ages but has fallen upon deaf ears.

We ask that you open your hearts and minds and look at what Nature has so graciously laid out before you, for through this incomparable vision, you will be transformed. Too numerous to mention, Nature has provided miracle upon miracle in the frequency of divine love.

One example we shall bestow upon you is that of the cherished cetaceans. The whales and dolphins have continuously showered your planet with their unconditional frequency of love, as the Record Keepers and Guardians of the Earth, only to be hunted and slaughtered at the hands of man. These delightful, Blissful

Beings of supreme intelligence and love are the Vibrational Stewards of the Earth, embodying the stellar energetic frequencies that the planet will return to. They grace your plane from another star system to fulfill their duty of assisting the earthlings' emergence into The Golden Age of Light. They reside in the eleventh dimension and have sacrificed their existence to guide and awaken humanity, working diligently to repair and rebuild the electromagnetic grid and to raise the vibratory stature through their song.

As the Earth begins its *Return to Love*, we ask that you see the Spark of God in all Living Creation and embrace the uniqueness of All Beings, for every soul on your planet came here with the initial intent to awaken and evolve into a Higher Dimensional Being. Be in the LIGHT and breathe in the energies of LOVE and COMPASSION. Feel our warm embrace around you always, for we stand beside you as mankind redefines the Global Community of Higher Light Knowledge and you co-create A New Earth.

From the Solar Heart of Humanity, I bring you this message today. I AM Aurora.

AFFIRMATION

I AM choosing LOVE in every moment.

I AM welcoming the unique authenticity
of souls around me, joining together in a Unified Global Cause.

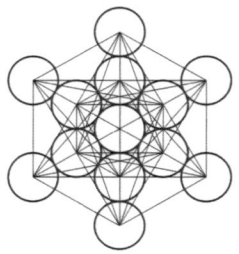

MORE
TRUTH
SHALL
SET
YOU
FREE

The seeds of consciousness are activated when you awaken to the realization that you are ONE with God, not separate from Source.

Modern-day religion has been misconstrued and twisted at the hands of man for personal gain and control of the masses. For this reason, many of the earthborn race have been turned off by "religion" and the strict constraints placed therein. What we would like to tell you, Dear Ones, is that the Heart of Spirit was never meant to be manipulated and dissolved in such a horrific manner, for God is All Loving, All Knowing, All Accepting. God does not control, connive, and twist, manipulating out of fear.

God does not threaten you and hover over you with an iron-clad weapon. God is LOVE, and God dwells in each and every one of you.

Inside each of you resides the I AM Presence, your Higher Self, which enables you to co-create with Source all that you desire. Every time you state I AM, you summon Spirit, God, Source, into motion, for within you dwells this Spark of Divinity.

Do you not feel the truth deep within your beingness as you read these words?

For this has been the biggest secret, known by few mystics, prophets, and seers through the ages. The secret is YOU ARE GOD. You are GOD. The Spark of God within you, your Higher Self, your I AM Presence, is the navigating, guiding force of everything in your life. And because you are ONE with God and All That Is, you are the architect of your reality. You are at the helm of your greatest dreams and visions, and the seeds of consciousness are activated when you open up to the understanding that you are ONE with Spirit, not separate from the Source.

We understand that when you initially read this, the realization may seem somewhat self-righteous and may even startle you, but as you affirm, "I AM One with God," you will feel the envelopment of Crystalline Light and Truth deep within your heart. We would ask that you joyfully claim this newfound birthright, for in doing so, you will experience tremendous peace, joy, compassion, love, and illumination.

We would also recommend that you work diligently on becoming a master of your thoughts and words, Beloveds, for the power of the spoken word is immense. Every time you utter or think a negative or damaging thought about yourself or another, you destruct and dismantle the I AM Presence within. Doubt erases your intuition and intention, and dampens the I AM Spirit, building a stone-clad fortress around your consciousness, limiting the conduit of light between you and the Universal Cosmic Field. We would, therefore, encourage you to *rearrange* your thoughts to be flooded with images and impressions of the ideals you wish to attain, experience, and achieve, for your mind is *Emblazed* with an imprint of all that you believe to be true.

Fill your cup with the I AM Teachings and affirmations—the *Elixirs of Light*, and you will not only transform yourselves but everyone you encounter.

So, Dear Ones, we ask that you emblaze these teachings deep within your beingness, for they will unlock the Secret Chamber of your Heart and ignite your vessel for Ascension. And so it is!

I AM Aurora, beside the Beings of Light and my beloved St. Germain, and we bring you these messages today.

AFFIRMATION

I AM One with GOD.

I AM a Keeper of the Flame,
a Master of my thoughts in each and every moment.

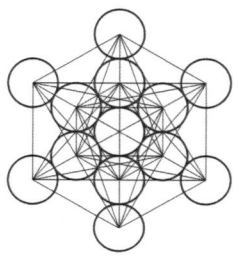

ALCHEMIZATION SYMPTOMS IN THE GOLDEN AGE

As you drop density and begin building your Body of Light, you may experience interesting physical symptoms.

As your physical body begins to drop density, there are many changes that occur within your framework. One of the most common sensations as you begin to build your light body is flushing or diarrheal episodes. You may suddenly have a four-day period of cleansing the intestines at different intervals during this process, for as you raise your frequency, your vessel must interiorly realign. It is as if you are going through an internal house cleaning, so to speak. You are in an ALCHEMIZATION process. Everything within your physical body is being recalibrated and realigned, similar to the overhaul of an old automobile.

Other symptoms you may experience are dizziness, spinning, blurred vision, extreme fatigue, insomnia, and headaches, to name a few. Your physical form needs time to integrate, assimilate, and anchor in these powerful high vibrational energies that are streaming through your beingness. You may feel dizzy or like the room is spinning when you stand up, lie down, or close your eyes. Fear not, for this is actually a very good sign that you are transmuting and transforming your flesh body into your Merkabic Throne Chariot.

There may be times when you feel like you have short-term memory loss, to the point of walking across the room and not remembering where you were going or what you were doing. You may stop mid-sentence, unable to form words. Remember, you are in a spiritual alchemical process. It is like an old house that has been stripped to the bare bones and is being remodeled.

You may feel extremely exhausted, no matter how much rest you're getting. Again, all part of the divine upgrade. Not only are you ANCHORING the new frequencies into your physical body and onto The Earth, but your system is also being fine-tuned and readjusted while you sleep. This allows for the rebuild to *settle in* and merge with your earthly vessel. It may feel as if there is a tingling, fiberoptic highway coursing through you when you lay down to rest.

The electronics in your home or surrounding area may suddenly go haywire or malfunction for no apparent reason. You may blow light bulbs and fuses. You may be driving under a streetlamp and notice it goes out, only to look in your review mirror and see it flash back on. The screen of your television set may turn grainy when you pass by or are in close proximity to it. This is because as your frequency rises, you emit extremely high-velocity electromagnetic pulses that affect the electronic devices in your energetic vicinity. As frustrating as this may seem, it is actually a fabulous sign that your vibration is very high! Try to see the humor and gift in it!

Additional symptoms we would like to include are severe occipital headaches at the base of the skull near the *Mouth of God*. This is an extremely sensitive area on your vessel, located where your head sits on your spinal column that pulls in higher light energy. So, if the pressure becomes too great, press your thumb firmly in the divot and ask that the pain subside. Small episodes of racing heart, like butterfly wings, may also occur as you re-activate your light body. This is very brief but can grab your attention. The multifaceted jewel of the heart is opening and expanding more fully in preparation for deeper communication through your heart center as a multidimensional being.

Dear Ones, we ask that you have faith and try not to be alarmed by these temporary and transitory feelings and sensations taking place in your physical form, for they, too, are in accordance with your cosmic upgrade and movement forward into your perfected crystalline light bodies. Added benefits of shifting into the light body are age reversal and disappearance of pain in the physical vessel.

Please also understand, Beloveds, that it is not our intention to diagnose or give medical advice. We are simply explaining various physical sensations that may temporarily arise as you raise your vibration and maximize your light quotient. We are not asking you to blatantly ignore physical pain, for what we are speaking of is very short-term and fleeting. If you are experiencing substantial, intense physical discomfort for any reason, we would encourage you to seek out assistance for appropriate health care monitoring.

We are the Beings of Light and Aurora, and we love you deeply.

AFFIRMATION

I AM upgrading my merkabic matrixes,
integrating and assimilating all that I AM.

I AM Alchemizing
and re-igniting my perfected Body of Light now.

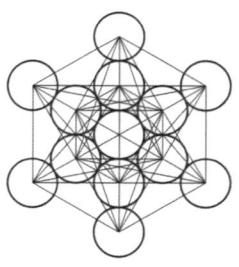

BE
NOT
AFRAID

Be not afraid, Dear Ones. We will always appear in the LIGHT, and you will feel Love, Compassion, and Serenity radiating from our energy fields.

What we would like to tell you, Beloveds, is that there have been forces of dark that have attempted to scare humanity through negative films and media, creating horrific aliens and reptiles coming through the sky in crafts and UFOs on the big screen, so to speak. The dark forces have attempted to paralyze the masses through fear to prevent a warm reception for us—The Beings of Light, The Sky Borne Command of The Most Radiant One, for we are not of those races.

We have protected your planet for many centuries from undue harm by negative races and authority figures. We have detonated nuclear missiles, atoms, and bombs to protect your planet's existence. We feel a deep connection to the human race, and it is our urgent mission to assist in the long-awaited Ascension and entrance into The Golden Age.

The new waves of crystalline light showering your planet bring the ultimate level of peace and joy for Mankind. *LOVE* will be the universal password, and the energy of Freedom and Bliss will be experienced at a level never before imagined. You will communicate through mental telepathy and the multifaceted jewel of the heart. The days of emotional upheaval will soon come to an end, and you will experience love in its grandest form. The Light has already won.

We look forward to our most blessed reunion with our Earth families soon. KNOW that your Star Families are near you, always protecting you, as they patiently await your joyful reunion.

In loving service, I AM Aurora.

AFFIRMATION

I AM releasing and removing any fear, negativity,
any unhealthy or destructive images
or beliefs, negative implants, chips, machinery, or encryption
from ALL levels of my Beingness
and my cellular memory NOW and forevermore.

I AM holding the TORCH OF LIGHT for humanity to awaken!

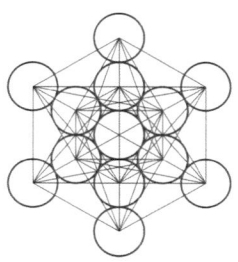

RETURN
TO
LOVE

Earth is beginning its Return to LOVE. In the new fifth-dimensional reality and beyond, nothing less than love shall exist, for within the new domain of Terra resides the frequency of pristine purity.

The Golden Age of Light that you are preparing to enter will exist on a level and frequency of Christos UNITY Consciousness, or Christ Consciousness. We ask that you follow and honor your inner gauge as you continue to build your perfected Body of Light, for in doing so, all will unfold into The Aquarian Age.

We ask that you love ALL your brothers and sisters on Earth, even those that are *asleep*, for they too have vowed to come to this plane with the initial intent of basking in the light of Spirit.

As you see the Spark of God in All Creation, you awaken to the higher dimensional aspect of YOU, and your Higher Self emerges, showering unconditional love and compassion upon everyone you meet. This energetic exchange penetrates the souls of those around you, even if not visually apparent, which in turn gives them permission to awaken and REMEMBER the ancient memory of who they are and their unique purpose on Earth.

So, Beloveds, share your light and wisdom with everyone you meet, for it will create a profound ripple effect and provide a mystical clue in the spiritual evolution of others as you joyfully co-create The New Earth.

We are the Beings of Light and Aurora, beside The Most Radiant One, in divine service and love always.

AFFIRMATION

I AM a TRANSMITTER
of crystalline light frequency.

I AM a Beacon of Light,
radiating love to all I meet.

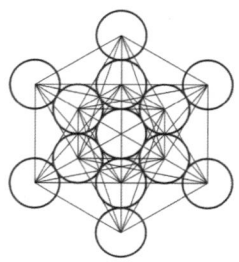

ETHERIC
HEALING
SQUAD

You each have an Angelic Healing Team that assists you in your physical, emotional, and spiritual recalibration and healing during your Ascension process.

Each of you reading these pages has come here to assist the planet in its transition, whether you consciously realize it or not. As such a member of the Earth Allegiance of Light, you are assigned an etheric healing squad, or angelic healing team, that works with you upon request. These are extremely loving Beings, a conglomeration of Angels, Star People, Ascended Masters, Elementals, and other Cosmic Guides.

We ask that when you are ready to go to sleep at night, you lay comfortably on your back with your arms at your side and call in your etheric healing team. You will be presented with a name for this special group; do not judge it when it comes to you; it may be playful or serious—nevertheless, it will appear.

Tell these Beings what is going on in your physical body, what hurts or aches, and what you would like them to heal. They do not need to hear specific diagnostic terms, as medical diagnosis imprints negative energy into your blueprint. Then THANK them! As you drift off to sleep, you will feel tingles and other airy sensations going on throughout your vessel. You may also feel your body begin to vibrate as if there's a fiberoptic highway coursing through you.

As Light Servers, your systems need extra energy and attention due to all of the gridwork, anchoring in of frequencies, and coding you provide to the planet and others each day. Some nights, you may want to simply ask for a good night's sleep, and to feel rejuvenated and energized upon awakening. You may also ask for emotional, mental, and spiritual healing. No request is too small or large, for these Beings have vowed to be with YOU, at your service in divine love and light, just as you have vowed to be here and assist Mother Earth.

In adoration and light, I AM Aurora.

AFFIRMATION

I AM grateful for my Etheric Healing Squad
and thank them for my stellar health now.

I AM whole. I AM happy. I AM healthy. I AM healed!
Every cell in my body is in pristine perfection now.

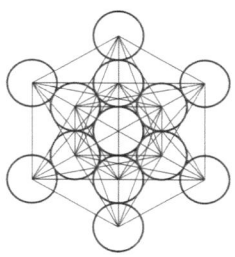

CITIES
OF
LIGHT

Intergalactic Cities of Light. The way of the future in the new Era of Terra.

There are Intergalactic Cities of Light above you, with Cosmic Beings existing on a different dimensional plane of supreme wisdom and intelligence. These cities in the sky are located directly above you and when you are vibrating at a higher velocity, you will be able to see our silver chariot cities with intergalactic buildings and architectural delights.

We have chosen to be above you at this time to monitor your energies and evolution, and to provide you with the necessary downloads needed in order to raise the planet's frequency and assist in ushering you more fully beyond the veil into The

Golden Age. There will be a time soon, in days ahead, when we will walk beside you and co-exist in peace, honor, and love for ALL.

As the Earth shifts into its new SPHERICAL reality, mankind opens the doorway to higher dimensionality, co-creating unity and harmony for All Beings throughout the Galaxies as we joyfully celebrate an unprecedented Intergalactic co-existence throughout the Cosmos.

As your dedicated Servant of Light, I AM Aurora.

AFFIRMATION

I AM igniting the codes and filaments of light
stored deep within my Beingness now.

I AM a Luminous Being of Light,
vibrating in my highest frequency in every moment.

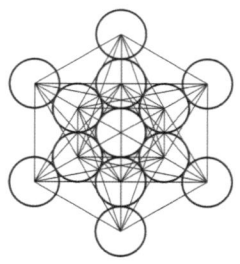

CLARION
CALL
WITHIN

As you awaken to the call within, you join the Legions of Light and become a precious link in co-creating A New Earth.

We ask that you don your Radiant Robes of Light and join the unified efforts of the Air Fleet Command of The Most Radiant One, beside the Beings of Light and myself, AURORA, to assist in this most vital mission on Planet Earth. The time is now to activate within, to share your light, understanding, and teachings with the world at large.

The entrance and unfoldment beyond the veil will happen in a building or layering effect, for there is no *light switch* moment. It will take some time for the upgraded spherical energies to settle into The New Earth, for the Ascension of the planet is a gradual process, and the Earth will take time to integrate the new energies of The Aquarian Age.

We ask that you stay the course beside us and hold the field, assisting Mother Earth and her inhabitants as they integrate the petals, diagrams, and layers of sacred geometry, beautifully showering the plane as your planet enters The Golden Age.

Each of you reading these pages has received the *clarion call* within to step forward and join the Legions of Light as we move most graciously into the new Era of Terra. Many have been called but have ignored the inner prompting. Some have gotten too distracted with the everyday events of their third-dimensional lives and have chosen not to listen. Some have ignored the inner prompting to turn inward, to bask in the energies of divine knowingness, and to feel the presence of The Great Teachings. We hold these souls in our hearts and await the day that they, too, may be awakened to the Light of Spirit.

But for you now, we honor and applaud you, for you have answered the call and have abided by the Laws of Spirit at this most urgent time on the planet. We ask that you radiate your glorious essence to everyone you meet, to tell your story of awakening to all who will listen, to joyfully speak to your friends, family, and acquaintances, for it is through these communications that others will ignite their light within. And so it is!

We applaud you greatly, Dear Ones, for you vowed to come to Planet Earth at this time, to embrace the opportunity to be a Broadcaster of Light, to set energetic templates, and raise the vibrational frequency of all you meet through your words, voice, creative talent, service, and song. For this, we tremendously honor you.

In infinite gratitude, I AM Aurora.

AFFIRMATION

I AM a BROADCASTER of Light.

I AM answering the Clarion Call within
and fulfilling my mission on Earth.

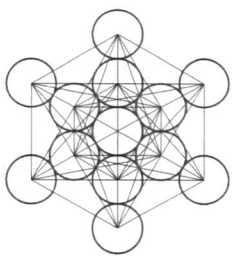

INTERGALACTIC HEALING CHAMBERS

Intergalactic Healing Chambers in the new Era of Terra.

Dear Ones, we invite you to enter our Light Synthesis Healing Chambers at night, when you have laid down to rest, for we assist you in your healing and rejuvenation process. For those of you who are guided, we ask that you call upon the Christed Cosmic Healing Chamber of Light to assist you in upgrading your light quotient, healing your physical distress, and assist in your light body recalibration process. For through this portal, you will be healed.

In future days, there will be light-filled healing chambers, tangibly located throughout the Cities of Light, as you emerge on the other side of The Golden Age and continue to assimilate the powerful energies of The New Earth. It will take some time to hold the monumental amount of light that will be available on the planet and these chambers are a way to fully integrate and maintain the new intergalactic frequencies.

In infinite devotion, I AM Aurora.

AFFIRMATION

I AM infused with the Golden Liquid Light
of the Christed Cosmic Healing Chamber now.

I AM upgrading my light quotient now!

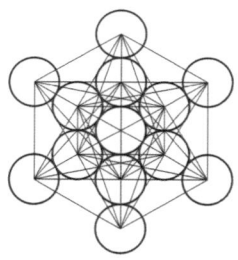

COSMIC COMMUNICATION

Intergalactic Communication We are with you ALWAYS!

Look into the night sky, and you shall see us. When you open up to our communication and clarity, we are there. We may appear as a twinkling light or a white light that glistens and disappears. We may appear as a large sphere that glides quickly across the sky or in our Christed Chariots coming in close. We have also been known to move around in a *sprinkling* effect or appear as ORBS.

We would like to make your acquaintance and let you know that we are here on a Christed Christos Mission and always have been. The thinning layers of recent times have allowed us to make communication with you more clearly. This opening has made it easier for us than in the past.

There will be days in the future when you may hear tapping, clicks, or, as you say, *morse code* in one of your ears. You may also experience substantial ringing or a marked humming that can be quite prevalent. These are all ways that we tell you we are present and would like to make contact.

So, we would ask at these times that you stop what you are doing, sit down quietly, and open up to our loving insight and communication. This will be channeled knowledge that flows easily and effortlessly through you. Some of you have already experienced this gift and are assisting humanity on a large scale with the information you have transcribed. Some have shared their messages with mankind through writing, song, film, or other forms of creative expression and talent to reach the masses.

We salute you all! We are entering the glory days, and the glory days will be divine, for you are exalted in your dedication and service to the planet.

I AM Aurora.

AFFIRMATION

I AM communicating clearly
with the Cosmic Beings of Light that guide me.

I AM a clear channel of light and knowledge.

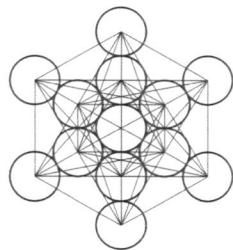

EMERGENCE
OF
LIGHT

Light emerging beyond the veil.

Structure, as it is known to Man, is no longer tangible. Humanity must now turn inward and discover the greater dimensional reality of *Self* in order to evolve and advance beyond the veil in this unprecedented time on the planet. Structure is changing and can no longer be measured solely by scientific methods, studies, and interpretations.

The Earth plane is continuously inundated with petals, diagrams, sacred geometrical structures, crystalline light, and orbs that beautifully shower the planet unceasingly. It is now time to merge with this divine intelligence, to awaken to the INTERCONNECTEDNESS of All That Is, and to bask in the knowingness that you are majestic Multidimensional Beings capable of creating all that you desire.

The energies you will integrate as you cross the veil into The Golden Age and traverse through the sacred geometrical matrixes of light, recalibrate and realign your vessels through the multifaceted crystalline structure within the Secret Chamber of your Heart. We are here in service as your Brothers and Sisters of Light, available at any time to infuse your bodies with energy blessings from the stars. Ask, and you shall receive, Dear Ones! Open up to the pure infusion of Diamond Crystalline Light, and your systems will be upgraded and restored. As you receive these Ascension Blessings, the multifaceted jewel of the heart ignites at an ancient core level. Everywhere you go, everyone you meet will feel the luminous Light of Spirit emanating from your newfound frequency as you expand and awaken the hearts and minds of all.

So, Beloveds, do not lose sight of your missions, for each of you is an intricate piece of the puzzle, placed on Earth at this exact time to perform a particular task that only YOU can fulfill with your exquisite, unique energy. As you honor your soul's splendidness, you shine light on humanity, the galaxies, and BEYOND, for you are Temples of Living Light, Emissaries, and Guardians of The New Earth.

As your faithful Messenger of Light, I AM Aurora.

AFFIRMATION

I AM receiving Energy Blessings from the Stars now.

I AM a trusted EMISSARY of Light and Guardian of The New Earth!

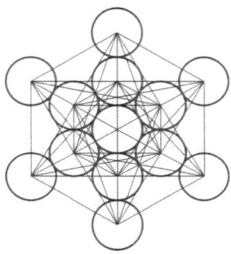

JOYOUS REUNION

We hold you in our hearts!

Through the Air Fleet Command of The Most Radiant One, we serve you. The joy in our hearts is immense, for you have stepped forward and answered the clarion call within. We surround you with many celestial crafts in the sky, too numerous to count, fine-tuning and upgrading your energies. We patrol your planet, faithfully upholding our mission to assist the Earth in its entrance into the new Age of Light.

We appear to you and communicate with you through our heart centers, always guiding and assisting you. We look forward to the day when we are able to fully decloak our silver chariots in the sky so that ALL will know our presence of Spirit. When we shall walk hand-in-hand as Brothers and Sisters of Light, building and expanding our Cities of Light in the most-anticipated Heaven on Earth.

We hold you in our hearts ALWAYS and so greatly honor you for your service and unwavering dedication in the role you came here to fulfill, as you have been a *precious link* in rewriting the history of the Cosmos forevermore.

In infinite love and service, I AM Aurora.

AFFIRMATION

I AM a precious link,
assisting in the mass awakening of humanity!

I AM a Temple of Living Light,
multidimensional and fully activated!

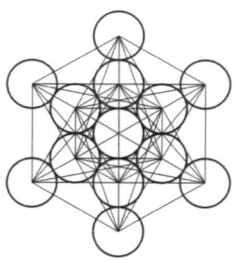

MESSAGE
FROM
AURORA

As Aurora of Light, I come to you from a Sister Galaxy of Christos Crystalline Unity Consciousness, bringing you messages of Peace, Faith, and Love. I work primarily from the ninth through twelfth dimensions at the right hand of The Most Radiant One, assisting all who wish to heal, transmute, and Ascend. From our vantage point, we see the earthlings struggling to attain the light of consciousness, negating their circumstances through self-sabotage and fear. Have faith, Children of Light, for it is your divine destiny to walk hand-in-hand in the Light of Spirit, where ALL things are possible, as you most magically create the long-awaited Heaven on Earth, and your beautiful planet evolves *beyond the veil* into The Golden Age.

I AM Aurora, and I AM honored to serve you and your beloved planet. I have guided many through their journeys into the light, and I am a specialist in the field. I have manned the Starship of your Great Teacher Sananda, The Most Radiant One, and continue to work by his side, assisting many souls and races in their healing, awakening, and transmutational process.

We ask that you now join hands with your Brothers and Sisters of Light as your beloved planet makes its leap into the cosmic circle of stars to join the other Star Nations and work together in creating the most majestic Heaven on Earth.

We ask that you bless and respect Mother Earth for the role she has so generously played throughout your incarnation on her plane, for she has faithfully supported and nurtured you as you have evolved through your personal dramas on the learning field. Your linear existence is but a brief blink in the grand scheme of the Cosmos. We ask now that humanity rise to the occasion, that you give thanks, bless, and love her magnificent essence for so faithfully holding the field for you in your long-awaited awakening and journey into the Union of Stars.

We rejoice and embrace all the members on Earth who have chosen to ride the wave of Unity Consciousness as you so diligently move into the Age of Aquarius, where there is perfect peace, harmony, and love for ALL Beings and ALL Planetary Nations. We unite with you in the stars and salute you for remembering your role in this grand celebration into the LIGHT.

I AM Aurora, in and through our beloved channel, Gia.

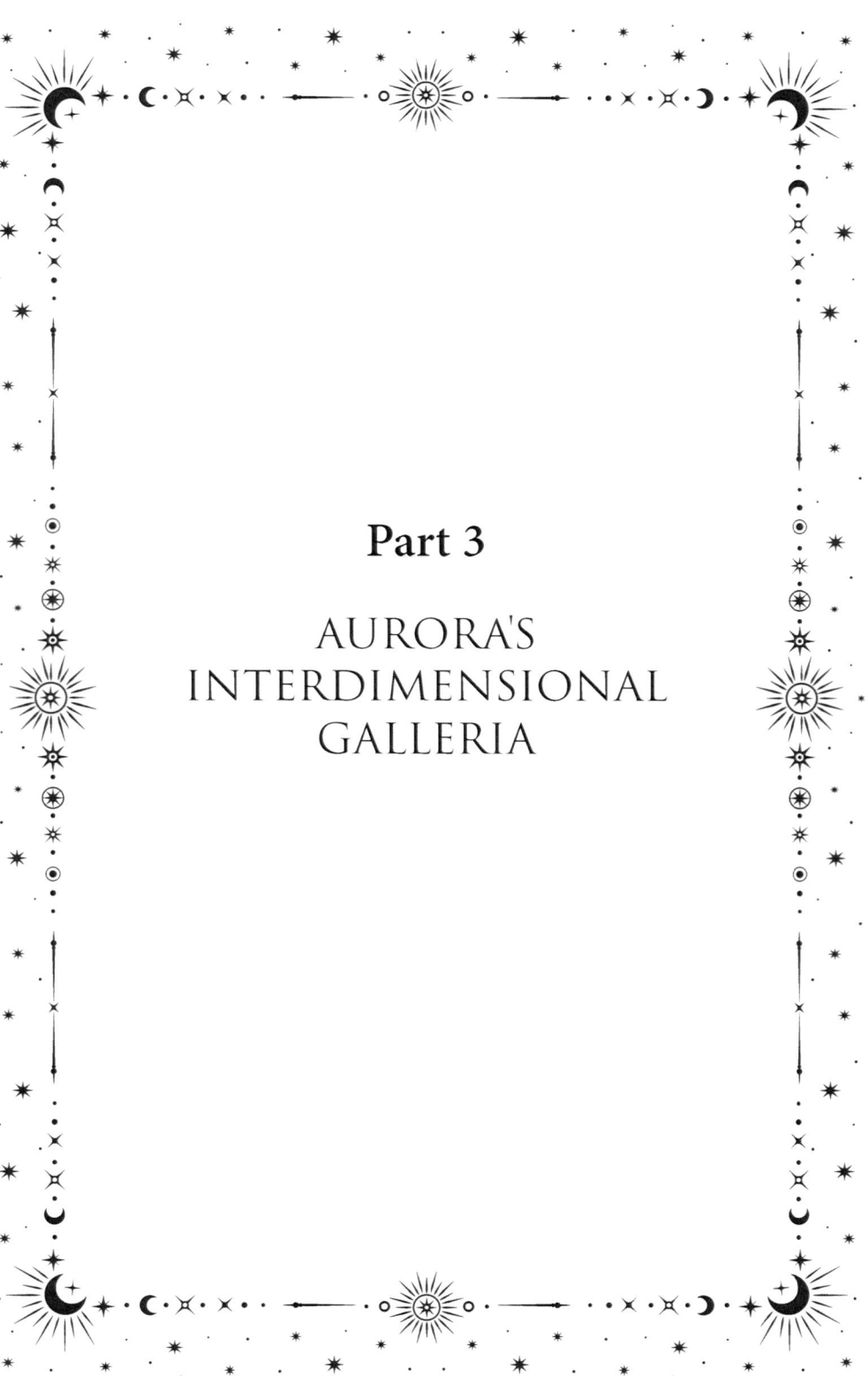

Part 3

AURORA'S INTERDIMENSIONAL GALLERIA

The following series of images are presented as an *Interdimensional Galleria* featuring AURORA and her Interstellar Collective in their unique cosmic expression. They change form and appear as plasma crafts, flying saucers, huge pastel orbs, opalescent orbs, rainbow orbs, opaque orbs, crystalline orbs, sparkling lights, orbs that shapeshift into flying saucers, ethereal humanesc light beings, and exquisite plasma crafts with sacred geometrical healing tools.

They also sometimes appear in the beautiful shades of the Aurora Borealis, or "inter-dimensional resonant tone." And, though they can and **do** travel in their crafts, they do not *require* them --they travel in their LIGHT BODIES and Orbs.

As you gaze upon the images in The Galleria, you receive divine downloads, awakening codes, keys, and filaments within, igniting the ancient memory of Who You Are as you raise your frequency and build your BODY OF LIGHT.

The photographic images were taken by myself or my daughter, Camille, some of which were captured with a camera while hiking, others spontaneously with a phone, and have not been edited.

I continue to have close encounters and interstellar experiences on any given day.

IMAGE 1

© Gia Govinda Marie

SEDONA, ARIZONA

Since my first trek to Sedona in 1997, I have felt an inner calling to return, an unparalleled prompting, to bask in the beauty of her essence and her majestic, mystical energy!

IMAGE 2

© Gia Govinda Marie

SEDONA, ARIZONA

While hiking with Camille on a clear spring day in Sedona, a large horizontal rainbow plasma craft began to emerge from behind the pine mountains. Emanations of energy and light are rising off the rainbow plasma craft in the center of this shot.

The energy was spectacular, radiating pastel pink, blue, and yellow, representing the three-fold-flame and Aurora.

I sensed there was much more going on and felt tingling all over my body, so I asked Camille to snap some quick, consecutive photos.

IMAGE 3

© Gia Govinda Marie

SEDONA, ARIZONA

Taken moments later, this image captures another view of the rainbow plasma craft rising from behind the pine mountains.

A Whirling Rainbow is beginning to appear above Aurora's three-fold-flame plasma craft. Knowing that the Whirling Rainbow promises PEACE among All Nations and All People, I understood the vision as a profound and urgent message of hope that Aurora and her Collective are bringing to humanity.

The "Whirling Rainbow" Native American prophecy states:

"There will come a day when people of all races, colors, and creeds will put aside their differences. They will come together in love, joining hands in unification to heal the Earth and all Her children. They will move over the Earth like a great Whirling Rainbow, bringing peace, understanding, and healing everywhere they go."[1]

1. No known copyright.

IMAGE 4

SEDONA, ARIZONA

This is a closer view of Aurora's three-fold-flame rainbow plasma craft. Seconds later, I was stunned to see Thorin, our beloved shepherd who had crossed over, appear in ethereal form, perched on top of Aurora's craft with the Whirling Rainbow above and behind him.

IMAGE 5

SEDONA, ARIZONA

Outlined view of Thorin's ethereal body perched on top of the three-fold-flame plasma craft.

IMAGE 6

Our beloved Thorin, who promised to make his ethereal presence undeniable.

IMAGE 7

SEDONA. ARIZONA

Another view of the Whirling Rainbow taken moments after Image 4. This photograph shows that the three-fold-flame plasma craft has shifted and is now tilting slightly to the left.

Thorin's etheric form is still perched on top of Aurora's plasma craft in front of the Whirling Rainbow.

IMAGE 8

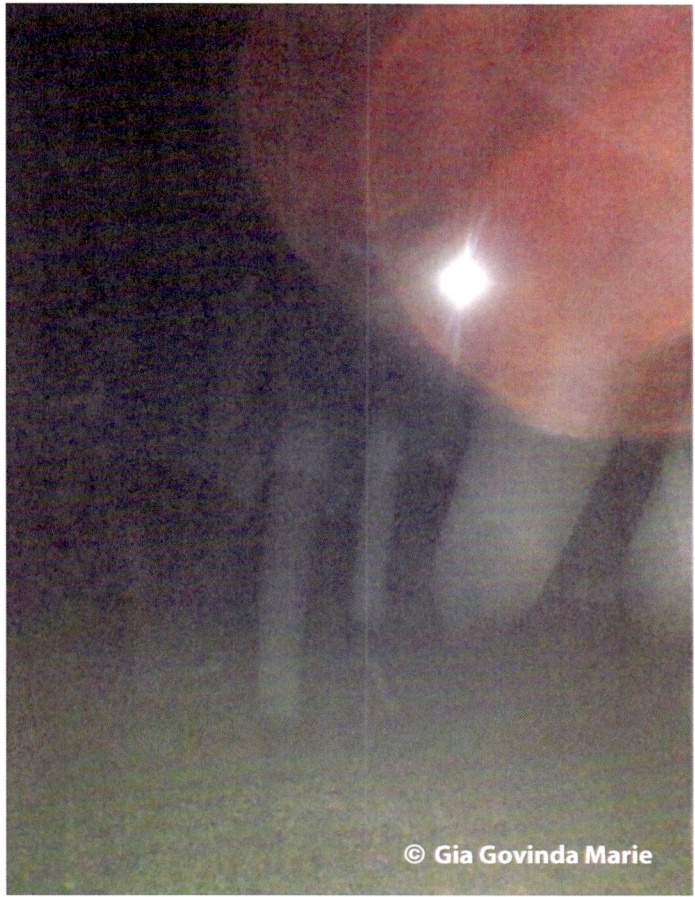

© Gia Govinda Marie

MIDWEST, USA

This image shows massive pink orbs in the meadow during a full moon, accompanied by crystalline pillar orbs.

Aurora also appears as crystal pillar orbs, as she and her Collective come from a Sister Galaxy of Christos Crystalline Unity Consciousness. They are *The Solar Crystal Temple Beings.*

The bright light on the left edge of the pink orb is the moon.

IMAGE 9

© Gia Govinda Marie

MIDWEST, USA

The massive pink orb shown in the previous photograph followed me as Gandalf, my shepherd, and I continued our late-night stargazing. Crystalline streams of light beam down, illuminating the doorway as we walked toward the cottage. An additional crystalline stream of light shines down directly in front of us.

Looking more closely at this image, I noticed what looks like the profile of a Light Being sitting inside the pink orb, possibly manning it as a craft.

Finn, the cat, is undisturbed by the intergalactic phenomena.

IMAGE 10

© Gia Govinda Marie

MIDWEST, USA

The massive pink plasma orb is now shining crystalline light into the side windows of the cottage.

The profile of a Star Being sitting inside the orb is more pronounced here, revealing that the Star Being appears to be navigating the plasma orb, as a beam of light shoots out from its third-eye area toward the cottage.

IMAGE 11

MIDWEST, USA

The massive pink plasma orb has moved closer to the cottage and is now beaming crystalline light into the upstairs windows.

IMAGE 12

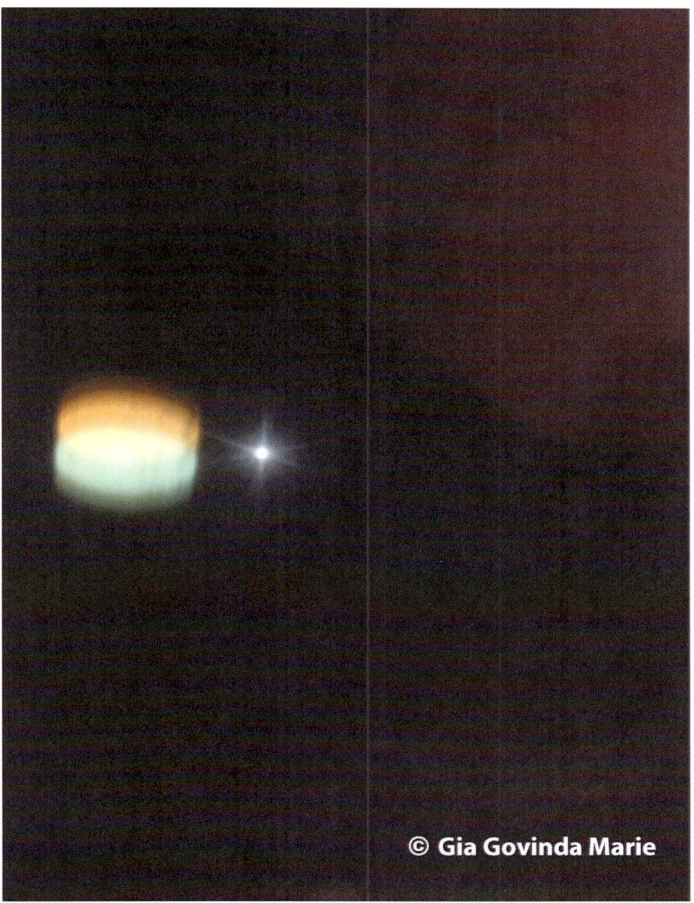

© Gia Govinda Marie

MIDWEST, USA

This photograph shows a pastel orange, yellow, and green plasma craft that appeared on the same evening during the full moon. The moon is the bright light to the right of the plasma craft.

The following images show the craft moving above the moon, then toward me, where I was standing.

IMAGE 13

© Gia Govinda Marie

MIDWEST, USA

The pastel orange, yellow, and green plasma craft has moved upward, as evidenced by its changed position in relation to the moon, which is now below and to the right of the craft.

IMAGE 14

© Gia Govinda Marie

MIDWEST, USA

This photograph captures the pastel orange, yellow, and green plasma craft moving toward me. The moon is now above and to the far right of the craft.

IMAGE 15

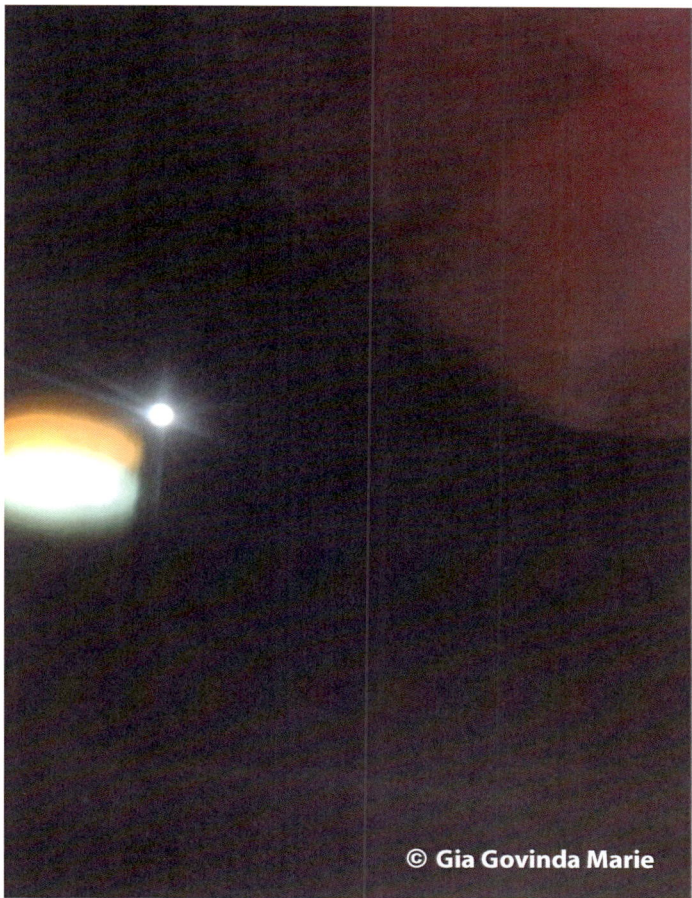

© Gia Govinda Marie

MIDWEST, USA

The pastel orange, yellow, and green plasma craft has moved even closer to me, with the moon appearing just above and to the right of the craft.

IMAGE 16

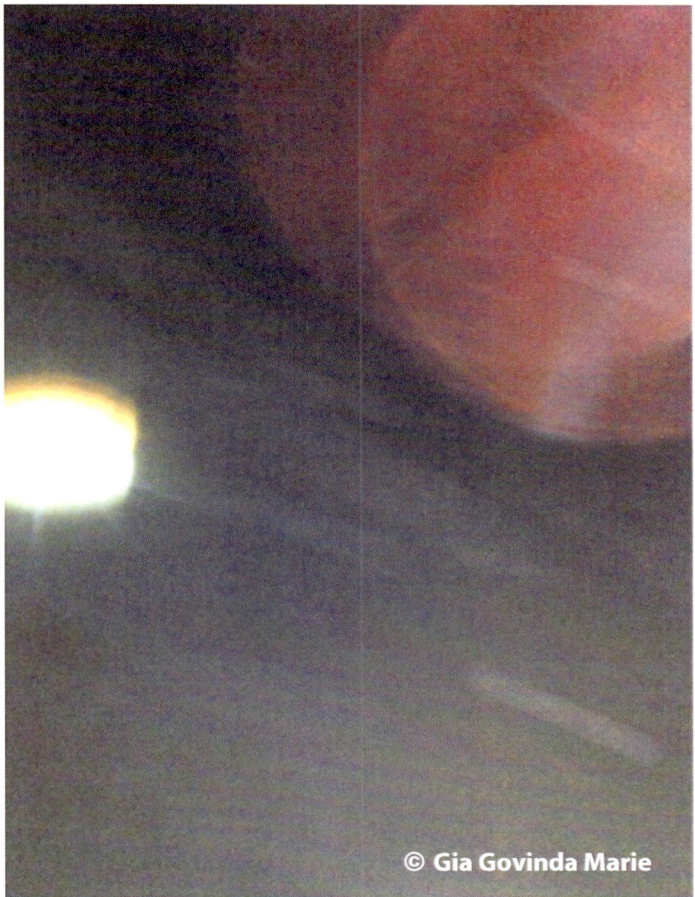

© Gia Govinda Marie

MIDWEST, USA

The pastel orange, yellow, and green plasma craft is now in close proximity to me, with the pink orbs shown in Images 8 through 11 reappearing. The closer the craft gets, the brighter it is, and it begins to glow.

Light emanations radiating out from the craft are seen below the massive pink orbs.

IMAGE 17

MIDWEST, USA

This is a beautiful sapphire plasma craft that appeared above the meadow one evening. It stayed with me for a while, and I was able to take a few more pictures of it.

IMAGE 18

MIDWEST, USA

As I was watching the beautiful sapphire plasma craft, a small white orb began to appear and glow beneath it, signifying the presence of a Light Being.

IMAGE 19

MIDWEST, USA

This photograph shows a massive orange, green, and yellow translucent orb moving behind the trees in the meadow where I was standing.

IMAGE 20

MIDWEST, USA

Seconds later, another view of the translucent orange, green, and yellow plasma orb, with a bright beam of light shooting down from the sky, signifying a craft or large starship above me.

IMAGE 21

MIDWEST, USA

Huge opaque mother-of-pearl plasma orb with a brilliant crystal pillar of light shooting down directly in front of me.

IMAGE 22

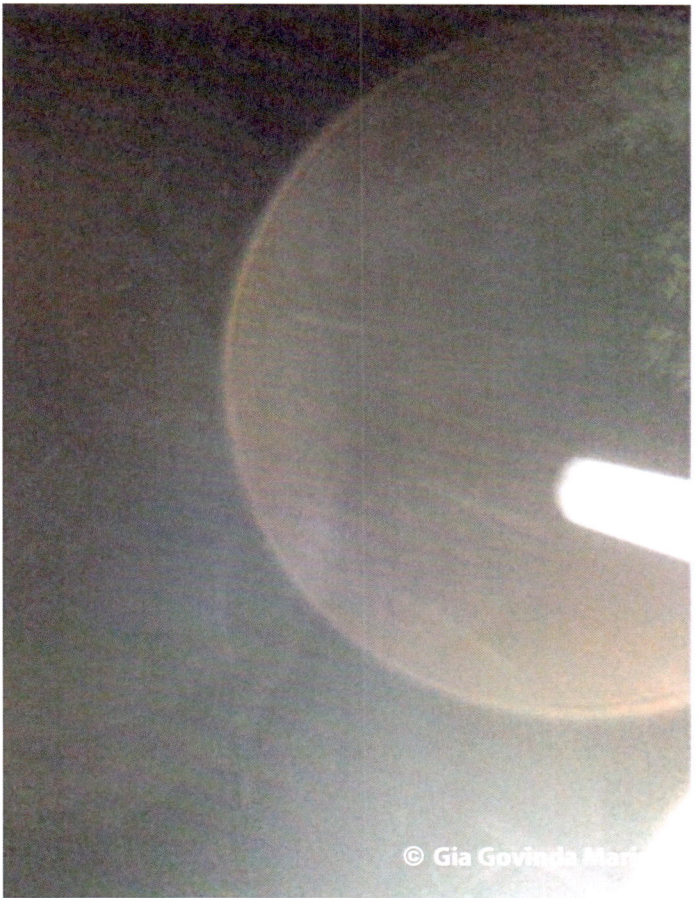

MIDWEST, USA

Massive opaque peach orb accompanied by a white tubular orb that appeared on the same evening as the previous photo. The peach plasma orb is changing color and beginning to shift into a flying saucer. The bright light in the bottom right corner of the photograph is a glowing craft coming in close.

Aurora and her Interstellar Collective easily shapeshift from orbs to flying saucers in a matter of seconds.

IMAGE 23

© Gia Govinda Marie

MIDWEST, USA

This silver-blue flying saucer approached me and Gandalf in the meadow on a late-night moonlit walk. I felt immense tingling and an energetic presence around me as the craft showered us with effervescent streams of crystalline light.

IMAGE 24

MIDWEST, USA

The silver-blue flying saucer in the top right corner began to change color as it rotated. As the flying disc spun, it became a more vibrant blue. The crystalline streams of light beneath the craft changed direction as my dog, Gandalf, and I looked on in wonderment.

IMAGE 25

MIDWEST, USA

This photograph shows a massive creamy mother-of-pearl orb with two additional opaque plasma orbs beginning to emerge from behind and above it while I was walking in the meadow on a beautiful fall night.

IMAGE 26

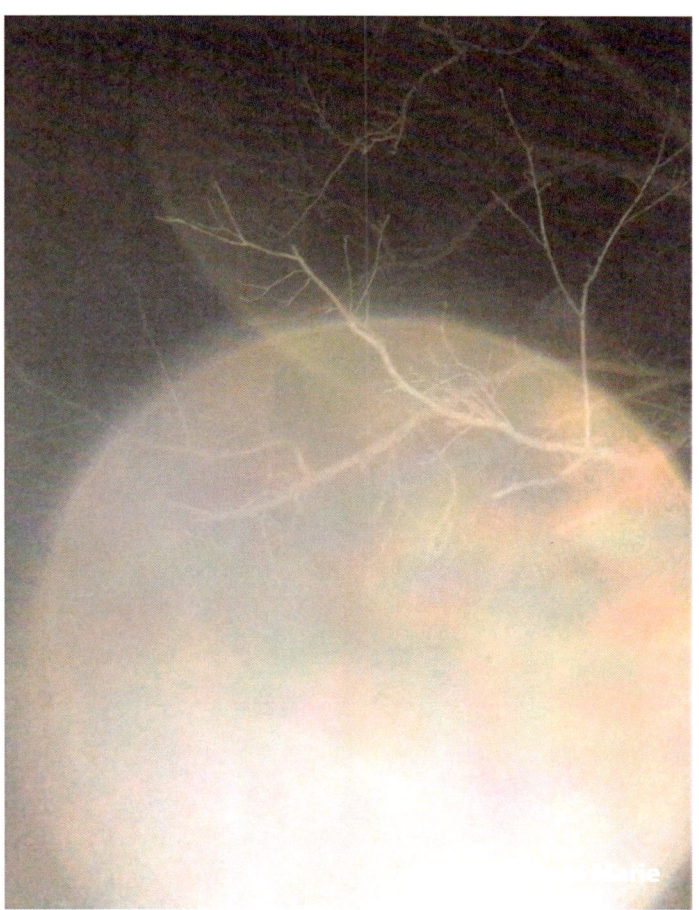

MIDWEST, USA

The massive creamy mother-of-pearl orb shown in the previous image followed me and moved through the trees. You can see the outline of an additional opaque plasma orb beginning to form above it.

IMAGE 27

© Gia Govinda Marie

MIDWEST, USA

Before Gandalf and I headed out for our moonlight walk, I called forth
Jesus and Aurora, asking them to upgrade my energy matrixes and
Crystalline Body of Light. To my delight, this huge golden orb appeared
above us with a beam of light shooting out to the right, seemingly
responding to my divine request!

IMAGE 28

MIDWEST, USA

The photograph shows the massive golden orb from the previous image as it accompanied us and moved through the treetops above.

IMAGE 29

MIDWEST. USA

This massive opaque pastel plasma orb, with tubular rainbow craft above it, appeared just before dusk on the Summer Solstice. You can see two large translucent orbs beginning to appear in the upper left.

There are two very tiny white orbs far off in the distance.

IMAGE 30

MIDWEST, USA

Beautiful cluster of pastel orbs that appeared in the cottage meadow. The white orb in the lower center is beginning to glow, signifying the presence of a Light Being.

IMAGE 31

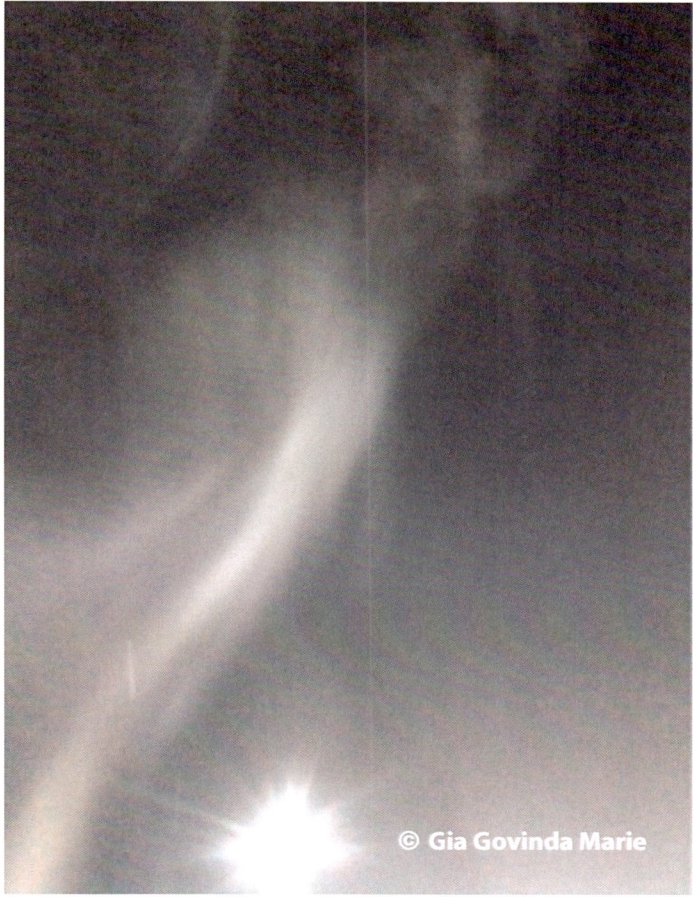

MIDWEST, USA

Taken seconds after Image 30, this photograph shows a faint, ethereal profile of Aurora Light Being as she appeared above Gandalf and me on our evening walk. You can see Aurora's faint facial outline, ear, hair, and flowing garment.

A large translucent plasma orb is just beginning to come into view in the upper left corner. The bright glowing light at the bottom center of the image is a full moon.

IMAGE 32

MIDWEST, USA

Taken moments after the previous photograph, this is a very faint profile of an Aurora Light Being in the upper right, with hair flowing and arms and legs outstretched, moving toward the opaque plasma orb in the upper left corner.

A bright full moon is shining in the lower center of the image.

IMAGE 33

MIDWEST, USA

Camille captured this huge cluster of white orbs above my head on my Birthday, as we sat under the stars and gazed at The Flower Moon.

White orbs generally signify the presence of Angels, Light Beings, purity and protection.

IMAGE 34

A unique art print of Jesus with his Ascension Halo. He is wearing his Robe of Light embossed with lilies and pearls as he emanates his teachings and blessings. There is a vajra pestle on his crown with blue lilies and lotus in his halo and energy radiating from his ears and head. It is a powerful image to gaze upon as you raise your vibration and build your Body of Light.[2]

Lilies are a symbol of resurrection, signifying hope and new life. Blue lilies are a divine connection to the Virgin Mary and the attainment of the impossible through perseverance. The lotus represents spiritual enlightenment. The craft-like halo around Jesus' head contains the blue and white lilies, lotus, and vajra pestles, representing the interconnectedness of Jesus' Resurrection Body of Light to the Tibetan Rainbow Body of Light. The pearls embossed on Jesus' garment signify divine wisdom, purity, and spiritual transformation. Indeed, a very powerful image to gaze upon.

2. Image credit and copyright unknown.

IMAGE 35

© Gia Govinda Marie

MIDWEST, USA

Just hours before taking this photograph, I invoked Padmasambhava, an enlightened Tibetan Being who has Ascended in his perfected Rainbow Body of Light, to assist me in building my own Rainbow Body of Light.

To my surprise, he made his presence known by appearing in light form, as the magnificent blue and golden orbs shown here above a cluster of huge opaque orbs.

IMAGE 36

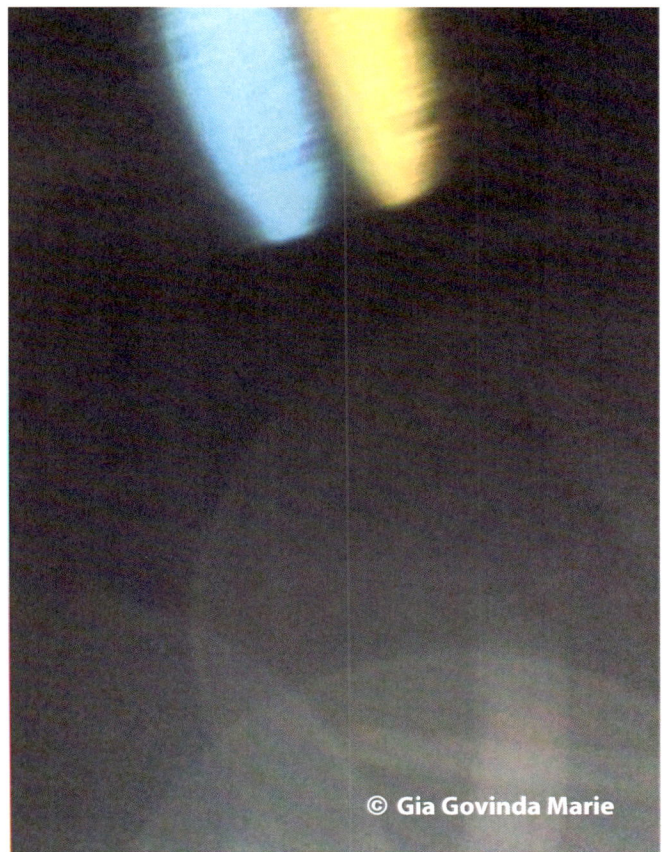

© Gia Govinda Marie

MIDWEST, USA

Padmasambhava's appearance after my invocation was even more astonishing when, seconds later, the pastel *crystalline cross* orb in the lower right of this picture appeared, signifying his connection to Aurora and the three-fold-flame!

Aurora works beside Jesus and the Ascended Masters, including Padmasambhava, assisting humanity in its awakening and Ascension process.

IMAGE 37

Framed print of Padmasambhava in his Rainbow Light Body that is very dear to me.[3]

Note the resemblance of frequency and colors to the blue and golden orbs reflecting Padmasambhava's vibrational essence, as well as the craft-like orb around him, which serves as his Merkabic Chariot, or Spiritual Vehicle of Ascension.

3. No known credit or copyright.

IMAGE 38

Prior to Padmasambhava's vibrational appearance. I had been frolicking in a meadow near the cottage. twirling in a circle with the beautiful rainbow blanket shown in this photograph. Without knowing it. I was channeling my inner whirling dervish. utilizing an ancient sacred devotional technique of spinning like a top to build my Rainbow Body of Light.

The "whirling dervish" symbolizes the journey of the Soul to God performed by the Sufi Ascetics and has been adopted throughout the centuries by many spiritual and religious affiliations. including the Tibetan and Zen Buddhists. as an Ascension Ritual.

I was profoundly moved when I made the connection between my whirling dervish playfulness and the appearance of Padmasambhava's light body later that day.

The wonders of Spirit never cease to amaze me!

IMAGE 39

SEDONA, ARIZONA

While taking a winter hike in Sedona, Camille and I stopped to rest and take in the beauty of nature. I noticed a small sapphire orb off in the distance and could sense a very strong, whirling, energetic presence in front of us. Camille had her phone in her backpack, so I asked her to click a few consecutive photos to see if anything would appear. She captured this image of me pointing in the direction of the energetic presence.

IMAGE 40

© Gia Govinda Marie

SEDONA, ARIZONA

The whirling energy quickly approached, and I could feel intense tingling behind me. It first revealed itself as small orbs, one sapphire and one peach.

IMAGE 41

© Gia Govinda Marie

SEDONA, ARIZONA

The two orbs shown in the previous image then moved to my left shoulder area.

IMAGE 42

SEDONA, ARIZONA

The interdimensional phenomena described in the previous two photographs continued to appear. In this image, a small sapphire-green plasma craft with sacred geometrical tool and laser tip begins to appear on my left. If you look closely, you can see the very faint outline of a white Light Being straight ahead, in front of the mountain.

I felt a very warm, immense amount of energy coursing through me during this encounter.

IMAGE 43

© Gia Govinda Marie

SEDONA, ARIZONA

The sapphire-green plasma craft shown in Image 42 moved behind my left shoulder and more clearly revealed a sacred geometrical pyramid laser with a partial white disk appearing beneath it. Prior to this, I had asked Aurora and the Beings of Light to heal my left shoulder and upper back from an injury I sustained while caretaking my woodland sanctuary.

I could feel tingling all around me. Camille could not see the energetic presence but continued to take photographs in my direction in hopes of capturing something on film.

IMAGE 44

SEDONA, ARIZONA

The sapphire-green plasma craft with sacred geometrical pyramid and laser from the previous two images increased in size, encompassing more of my left shoulder and upper back area, as shown in this photograph.

IMAGE 45

SEDONA. ARIZONA

The sapphire-green plasma craft with sacred geometrical pyramid and laser shown in the previous photographs then moved to the center of my upper back.

My neck was hurting from the shoulder injury: however. I did not mention this in my request for healing. Aurora and the Beings of Light were fully aware of the issue and made sure to provide aid!

IMAGE 46

© Gia Govinda Marie

SEDONA, ARIZONA

Closer view of the sapphire-green plasma craft with sacred geometrical pyramid and laser tool at the base of my neck and upper back.

IMAGE 47

© Gia Govinda Marie

SEDONA. ARIZONA

In this photograph, the sapphire-green plasma craft with sacred geometrical healing tool has enlarged itself and is more fully engulfing my upper back and left shoulder area.

IMAGE 48

SEDONA, ARIZONA

The sapphire-green plasma craft with sacred geometrical pyramid laser from the previous images has shapeshifted into an exquisite bell-shaped chariot with a bluish-white nucleus. A beam of blue light is shooting out from the pyramidal laser into my neck and head, where I was also having pain associated with the shoulder injury.

During this encounter, I was chanting affirmations and asking Aurora to upgrade my merkabic energy matrixes.

The bell-shaped plasma craft clearly signifies the Merkabic Throne Chariot, or Vehicle of Ascension.

IMAGE 49

© Gia Govinda Marie

SEDONA, ARIZONA

The bell-shaped chariot plasma craft shown in Image 48 has changed positions and moved to my left side.

I could feel a phenomenal amount of energy moving around me and an overwhelming sense of peace and serenity as Camille continued to click consecutive photos.

IMAGE 50

© Gia Govinda Marie

SEDONA, ARIZONA

As I stretched, the bell-shaped chariot plasma craft stayed by my side. This photograph and the series of images taken in Sedona on our winter hike all happened in a matter of moments as the sapphire-green plasma craft moved around me.

IMAGE 51

SEDONA, ARIZONA

The bell-shaped chariot plasma craft has moved closer to me on the left and is shooting a golden beam of light out of the sacred geometrical pyramid laser tip into my face, neck, and eyes.

I was chanting during this encounter, calling forth Christos Crystalline Diamond Light to upgrade my Merkabic Throne Chariot and build my perfected Body of Light.

IMAGE 52

© Gia Govinda Marie

SEDONA, ARIZONA

A light blue nucleus has appeared at the base of the sapphire-green bell-shaped chariot plasma craft. The pyramidal laser tip at the top of the craft is pointing directly at my face as I turn to the left, sending beams of indigo light into my third eye and crown area. The chariot plasma craft is also morphing and becoming more opaque.

I was continuing my chanting and had just called forth higher dimensional Christos Crystalline frequencies to assist me in upgrading my Merkabic Chariot and building my Body of Light. Camille was still clicking consecutive photos and could not see the interdimensional phenomena.

IMAGE 53

© Gia Govinda Marie

SEDONA, ARIZONA

The sapphire-green plasma craft from the previous images has shapeshifted into an even more elaborate chariot, with its sacred geometrical tool and pyramidal laser extending outside of its original circumference. If you look closely, you can see a tiny white orb that has appeared in front of my nose and third eye area.

As I turn to walk away, it follows me.

IMAGE 54

SEDONA, ARIZONA

I begin to walk away and resume hiking, and the sapphire-green chariot plasma craft, which has now shapeshifted into a small glowing orb, accompanies me.

IMAGE 55

SEDONA, ARIZONA

As I stop to look at rocks, the glowing sapphire-green orb is still with me.

After our winter hike in Sedona and the mystical encounter with Aurora and her Interstellar Collective, I had an overwhelming sense of peace. I was free from pain in my shoulder, neck, and head area.

"CELESTIAL ARRIVALS"

By Gilbert Williams

IMAGE 56

Shortly after my experience with Aurora and her chariot plasma craft, I came across a marvelous piece of art entitled "Celestial Arrivals" by Gilbert Williams.[1]

The resemblance to Aurora's sacred geometrical chariot craft tool is awe-inspiring and a powerful demonstration of the Benevolent Beings of Light among us!

I invite you to also note the light being, rainbow, glowing orb, plasma crafts, and emanation of divine light radiating from Source above.

1. Williams, Gilbert. "Celestial Visitations." The Art of Gilbert Williams (Celestial Arrivals). Pomegranate Artbooks 1979. Used with permission.

IMAGE 57

Author's rough sketch of AURORA.

"AURORA"

By Intuitive Artist, Steve Takes[5]

IMAGE 58

5. Used with permission.

I AM
the Embodiment
of Resurrection in this life.
I AM
the Victory of Freedom,
flowing freely and bright!

Gia Govinda Marie

ABOUT
THE
AUTHOR

Gia Govinda Marie is an Intuitive Healer, Teacher, Author, and
Interstellar Messenger who lives in the Midwest with her daughter,
beloved animals, and a menagerie of forest creatures in their enchanted
woodland sanctuary. As a noted leader in the field of Alternative
Medicine, Metaphysical Studies, and The Divine Human Potential,
Gia beautifully bridges Science and Spirituality, opening the doorway
for mankind to understand their Interconnectedness with All That Is

as we enter The Golden Age of Light. Her private healing arts practice encompasses Energy Medicine, Spiritual Counseling, Meditation, Light Body Activation, and communing with the Nature Spirits, Angels, Beings of Light, and Aurora. Gia has studied metaphysics for more than 30 years and dedicates her life to raising the frequency of the planet and assisting others in their healing, Conscious Awakening, and Ascension process. She travels the country, speaking and teaching, in an effort to raise awareness universally and assist all who wish to live their light, heal, and AWAKEN as we enter The Golden Age of Light, the new Era of Terra, and co-create A New Earth.

OTHER BOOKS
BY
GIA GOVINDA MARIE

"Being Light, Beyond the Veil of The Golden Age:
A Light Server's Guide to Harnessing the Energies of The
New Earth"
~An Ascension Tool~
(Balboa Press, 2015)

"Bejeweled Heart, Awakening the Light Within"
A Collection of Affirmations and Writings
to Assist Humanity's Awakening
into The Golden Age of Light
~A small daily companion~
(Llumina Press, 2009)

GLOSSARY

Angels

Very loving, higher dimensional Etheric Beings, also known as Messengers of God, who are here to protect, guide, comfort, and watch over the souls in embodiment on Earth.

Akashic Records

High vibrational ethereal imprint or library that chronicles the memory of everything that has ever occurred, in or out of embodiment, through all space and time. Every thought, feeling, word, deed, and impression is contained in this cosmic mirror and can be accessed through the development of psychic sight or inner vision. The Akashic Records contain the entire history of every soul, entity, and life form through the dawn of Creation, thus connecting us to one another.

Ascended Masters

Beings who have walked the Earth before, who have fulfilled their divine plan, mastered Self, and fully realized the I AM Presence of God within. They are ascended in the higher realms with the divine purpose of guiding and teaching humanity. (Examples: Jesus, Buddha, St. Germain, Kwan Yin, El Morya, Kuthumi, Apollo, Metatron, Melchizedek, Moses, Ashtar, and Mother Mary to name a few.)

Ascension (Planet)

The process of Planet Earth raising its dimensional frequency to a high enough vibrational state to be transformed into a star.

Ascension of Humans

A profound Awakening of Spiritual Consciousness within, which merges pure, divine, cosmic energy with the physicality of the human vessel, allowing humans to become ONE with God, Source Energy, and All Creation.

Aura

The electromagnetic luminous field of energy that surrounds an individual, Being, or object, which reflects our emotional, mental, physical, and spiritual health. The aura is a wide range of colors that can shift and change depending on one's mood, health, and emotional state of being.

Beings of Light

Light Beings, including, but not limited to, Angels, Ascended Masters, Elementals, Nature Spirits, Star People, and other Benevolent Cosmic Guides from various dimensions, galaxies, and star systems.

Buddha Nature

The innate wisdom of Siddhartha Gautama Buddha, which is genetically housed in each and every one of us, waiting to be uncovered, at which point we are gifted with deeper wisdom, peace, serenity, love, and compassion for all.

Cellular Memory

The cellular structure and complete memory blueprint within your genetic makeup that contains the database for ALL of your experiences, both positive and negative, through each and every lifetime, through all space and time. Every experience that has ever happened to you is stored in these cells. So, although you are incarnated on the Earth plane in THIS lifetime, your cellular memory is *susceptible* to, and may be *triggered by,* events you currently experience in this embodiment due to the ancient memory and knowledge contained therein. Once you are aware of this profound realization, you more easily integrate the understanding of Self and soar on your spiritual path.

Chakras

Vortexes or energy centers in the etheric body based on Eastern Philosophy. There are many chakras throughout the entire system, with the focus being on the seven main chakras from root to crown (although there are additional chakras that extend above the head and beyond.) The chakras correlate with the seven colors and seven notes on the musical scale, as well as the internal organs and endocrine system, and respond to our emotions, feelings, fear, and trauma. It is important to keep the chakras open and spinning beautifully to allow for the proper circulation of energy (chi, ki, prana) to flow through the physical body, allowing one to experience optimal health.

Children of Light

Those human beings who seek the Light and are being lovingly guided on their paths by Celestial Beings and other Cosmic Guides.

Christ Consciousness

The I AM Presence that dwells in each and every one of us, which awakens more fully upon the search for Light and Truth.

Christed Cosmic Crystalline Light

The purest essence of Light available to ALL life on Earth and All Beings throughout the Universes and Galaxies.

Christed ET's

Beautiful higher dimensional Star People that work in the Light beside The Most Radiant One to assist humanity and Planet Earth in its Ascension and transition into a star, carrying out God's plan for the Universe where there is perfect peace, love, and harmony for all.

Cosmic Angels & Beings

Advanced Beings from other Galaxies, Universes, and Star Systems who are here to help the human race heal, awaken, and evolve spiritually.

Creator

Another name for God, Spirit, Source, All That Is.

Crystalline Planetary Grid

Also known as Planetary Grid, Crystalline Grid, Christ Consciousness Grid, Grid of Light. This elaborate holographic higher dimensional crystalline matrix of light is linked to all of the major portals, vortexes, power spots, crystals, and cosmic doorways that connect the Earth to the Higher Dimensional Realms of Light, Galaxies, and Universes, ultimately creating an Intergalactic Bridge of Light. This Crystalline Grid serves as a "meridian system" for The New Earth, assisting humanity and All Beings in their healing, transformation, and transcendence into The Golden Age of Light, where there is peace, love, and unity among ALL.

Divine Blueprint

Your soul's own divine genetic library, spiritual guidepost, or chart that contains vast knowledge of your ultimate personal mission and purpose while incarnated on Earth, where you create understanding, fulfillment, abundance, love, and service to humanity. Your Divine Blueprint holds information from your Angels, Guides, Ascended Masters and Teachers, Elementals, and the God Source, Field, All That Is.

Etheric

Higher dimensional space beyond the Earth's atmosphere. Celestial Realm. Also known as ethers.

Elemental Kingdom

Nature Spirits, Fairies, Elves, Sprites, Gnomes, and other Beings living in the natural realms of Spirit as guardians of the earth, who lovingly care for Nature, wildlife, and all living things.

Frequency

The rate at which atoms and subparticles vibrate. Vibrating in your highest frequency brings you closer to Spirit, God, Source, your Buddha Nature, All That Is, and raises the consciousness of the planet.

Golden Age of Light

The coming Age of Light, also known as the Age of Aquarius, and New Earth, where Mother Earth and her inhabitants celebrate the ultimate level of Unity Consciousness, or Christos Christ Consciousness, where All Beings on Earth and throughout the Galaxies experience peace, love, and harmony for ALL.

Golden Liquid Light

Christed Cosmic Healing Light that flows from the higher dimensional atmosphere to all who request this profound healing energy.

Great White Brotherhood (White referring to LIGHT)

The Spiritual and Celestial Order of Cosmic Beings, Angels, and Ascended Masters united together for the highest purpose of God on Earth.

Gridwork

The unconscious act by Light Servers and Starseeds of setting energetic templates wherever they go. These templates assist the Earth in anchoring in higher light frequencies, which ultimately assist in the Ascension of the planet.

Higher Self

The I AM Presence, Divine Self, or Spark of God within, that is our true, exalted essence of self.

I AM Presence

The Spark of God within, the Higher Self.

Jewel of the Heart

Also referred to as Diamond Heart or Crystal Lotus Heart. The multifaceted crystalline structure of Christos Consciousness within the Secret Chamber of the Heart, which houses the keys to higher knowledge and your multidimensional self. It is activated upon spiritual awakening and serves as the navigation portal once the light body has been activated.

Keeper of the Flame

Those who have taken the vow to hold the violet flame of spiritual knowledge and transmutation within their hearts and utilize its profound energy to transform their lives and grow spiritually.

Light Body (Body of Light)

Your ethereal body in its perfected, superconscious state of being, which allows interdimensional communication and teleportation to other dimensional realities and spaces in time. Also known as Spiritual Body, Crystal Body, Diamond Body, Star Body, Radiant Body, Celestial Body, Resurrection Body, Rainbow Body, Crystalline Body, Adam Kadmon Body, and Christed Cosmic Crystalline Body of Light.

Light Servers

Incarnated souls who are awakening on Earth, working in the Light to carry out God's plan for the highest good of All Creation and Ascension of the planet.

Merkaba

The sacred geometrical energetic matrix that surrounds the physical vessel, which houses the codes and keys to the entire Universe and Galaxies. It is the Spiritual Vehicle for Ascension and space travel. Also known as Merkabic Chariot, Throne Chariot, Christos Chariot, Mystical Chariot, or Celestial Chariot.

Metaphysics

A branch of philosophy that applies the laws of physics to the spiritual world and the nature of reality, which exists outside of the human senses and time and space perception.

Multidimensional

Relating to or having several spatial experiences in different planes of energy.

Mutational Symptoms (Alchemization Symptoms)

Transitory physical sensations that occur in your physical vessel as you raise your frequency and shift more fully into your higher dimensional state of being and begin building your Body of Light.

Nature Spirits

The Fairy and Elfin Kingdom, also known as Elementals and the Nature Spirit Realm, that work in cooperation with Mother Earth for the highest good of All Beings. They nurture, watch over, and take special care of the Animal and Plant Kingdoms.

Orbs

Emanations of higher dimensional Spiritual Beings presenting in the form of sacred geometric shapes and symbols, which appear to be shimmering and floating, signifying the presence of Celestial Cosmic Beings, communicating and watching over you.

Orbs ~ Diamond-shaped

Christ Consciousness. God is present. Sacred place. Signifies higher dimensional work and communication with Celestial Cosmic Beings and Christed ET's.

Planetary Crystalline Grid

Also known as Crystalline Grid, Planetary Grid, Christ Consciousness Grid, Grid of Light. This elaborate holographic higher dimensional matrix of light is linked to all the major portals, vortexes, power points, crystals, and cosmic doorways that connect Planet Earth and her inhabitants to the higher dimensional Spiritual Realms, Galaxies, and Universes, ultimately creating an Intergalactic Bridge of Light, which assists All Beings in their healing, transformation, and transcendence into the new Age of Light, where there is peace, love, and unity for all.

Sananda

Another name for Jesus, The Most Radiant One. Sananda lovingly purifies the cathedrals and temples, removing manmade dogma, doctrines, and blatant manipulation of the sacred book, which has corrupted the purity of His teachings.

Secret Chamber of the Heart

The intimate sacred space, or spiritual treasure box within the heart, where Heaven and Earth reside and from where all creation emerges. The Secret Chamber houses the three-fold-flame of God and the jewel of the heart, or diamond heart.

Starseeds

Evolved individuals who originate from far-away star systems, planets, galaxies, and solar systems who have come to Planet Earth to assist the earthlings with their healing and conscious awakening process. These cosmic souls in human embodiment carry an exorbitant amount of knowledge, wisdom, gifts, and special abilities that lie dormant deep within their beingness until their galactic genes ignite a "wake-up call" coding, which enables them to activate at a predetermined time in their incarnation to assist humanity's transfiguration, transcendence, and Ascension into The Golden Age of Light.

Teleportation

The method of being transported across distance and space instantly in a higher dimensional state of energy, using thoughtform, light, and the light body.

Templates

Energetic matrixes set in the Earth that allow higher light frequency from solar flares, astrological alignments, or other cosmic events to enter the planet, assisting Mother Earth in her Ascension process.

Terra

Another name for Planet Earth, subsequent to her transition into a star and emergence into The Golden Age of Light.

The Most Radiant One

Master Jesus, also known as Sananda throughout the higher dimensional realms. He is a member of the Great White Brotherhood and mans the Star Borne Fleet, overseeing the

Great Shift as Mother Earth Ascends and humanity awakens and enters The Golden Age of Light.

Third Eye

The psychic eye, or intuitive center, located between the eyebrows in the middle of the forehead. The third eye is the 6th chakra, and upon activation through meditation, spiritual practices, and communing with God, Source, All That Is, produces extrasensory perception.

Three-Fold-Flame

The Divine Spark within, residing in the Secret Chamber of the Heart. The three flames, which are blue, yellow, and pink, represent the Heavenly Trinity, expressing the energies of Father, Son, and Holy Spirit. This flame is the essence of God, Spirit, Source, your Buddha Nature, All That Is.

Vibrational Frequency

The velocity at which atoms and subparticles vibrate in an individual or entity. The higher the vibrational frequency, the closer one is to the Light, God, Source, their Buddha Nature, All That Is.

Violet Flame

The violet flame of spiritual transmutation, which assists an individual in transforming all areas of their life and awakening spiritually. Ascended Master St. Germain gifts humanity with the teachings and understanding of the violet flame.

Vortex

Amplified places of energy that serve as powerful entrance and exit portals of the Planetary Crystalline Grid System, wherein high vibrational spiritual energies flow back and forth beyond the Earth, space, and time.